747.09046
S625
20

D1033560

Art Center College of Design
Library
1700 Lida Street
Pasadena, Calif. 91103

COLLECTOR'S COMPASS™

'60s and '70s Decor

Martingale™
& COMPANY

ART CENTER COLLEGE OF DESIGN

3 3220 00265 8149

Credits

President . . . . Nancy J. Martin
CEO . . . . Daniel J. Martin
Publisher . . . . Jane Hamada
Editorial Director . . . . Mary V. Green
Editorial Project Manager . . . . .Tina Cook
Series Editor . . . . Christopher J. Kuppig
Copy Editor . . . . Allison A. Merrill
Design and Production Manager . . . . Stan Green
Series Designer . . . . Bonnie Mather
Production Designer . . . . Jennifer LaRock Shontz
Series Concept . . . . Michael O. Campbell

Collector's Compass™: '60s and '70s Decor
© 2001 by Martingale & Company

Martingale & Company
20205 144th Avenue NE
Woodinville, WA 98072-8478 USA
www.martingale-pub.com

Printed in Canada
06 05 04 03 02 01   6 5 4 3 2 1

On the cover: Cantilever chair, Verner Panton design, vintage example manufactured by Herman Miller (U.S.A.), ca. 1972. TR-005 Orbitel TV, Panasonic, 1970. *Photos courtesy of Erica George Dines.*

All rights reserved. No part of this book may be reproduced without written permission from the publisher, nor may any part of this book be reproduced, stored in a retrieval system, or transmitted in any form or by any means—electronic, mechanical, photocopying, recording, or other—without written permission from the publisher.

The information in this book is presented in good faith, and while every precaution has been taken in the preparation of this book, the publisher assumes no responsibility for errors or omissions. The publisher disclaims any liability in connection with the use of this information. For additional information please contact Martingale & Company, 20205 144th Avenue NE, Woodinville, WA 98072-8478.

Library of Congress Cataloging-in-Publication Data
'60s and '70s decor.
p. cm. — (Collector's compass)
Includes bibliographical references.
ISBN 1-56477-378-7
1. Plastics in interior decoration—United States. 2. House furnishings—Collectors and collecting—United States. 3. Nineteen sixties—Collectibles. 4. Nineteen seventies—Collectibles. 5. Design—Italy. I. Title: Sixties and seventies decor. II. Series.

NK2115.5.P5 A13 2000
684'.0075—dc21   2001022251

Mission Statement

We are dedicated to providing quality products and service by working together to inspire creativity and to enrich the lives we touch.

Art Center College of Design
Library
1700 Lida Street
Pasadena, Calif. 91103

CONTENTS

FOREWORD

As America's favorite hobby, collecting is exciting, gratifying, and above all, fun—but without the right knowledge, you could be destined for disappointment. Luckily, you've just found the most resourceful and inspiring series of guidebooks available to help you learn more about collecting. The Collector's Compass series approaches collecting in a whole new way, making it easy to learn about your favorite collectible categories—from the basics to the best-kept secrets.

The International Society of Appraisers (ISA) is pleased to be associated with the Collector's Compass series. As the ISA celebrates twenty years of professional education and certification of personal-property appraisers, who currently specialize in more than two hundred areas of expertise, we remain committed to setting the highest standards for our accredited members. The Collector's Compass series of reference books reflects the ISA's dedication to quality and integrity.

Christian Coleman, ISA CAPP, Retired
Executive Director, International Society of Appraisers

Art Center College of Design
Library
1700 Lida Street
Pasadena, Calif. 91103

INTRODUCTION

Whether it means setting the alarm clock for Saturday morning yard sales, watching *Antiques Roadshow,* or chasing down childhood memories on eBay, collecting has become America's favorite hobby. The joy of finding treasure amid the clutter of a tag sale or a screen full of online offerings is infectious. Who could resist a pastime that combines the fun of shopping, the thrill of the hunt, the lure of a bargain, and the pride of ownership?

Throngs of novice collectors are joining experienced veterans in online bidding and weekend antiquing expeditions. If you count yourself among them, this book is for you.

The editors of the Collector's Compass series realized that today's collectors need more information than what was then obtainable, in an accessible and convenient format. Going beyond available price and identification guides, each Collector's Compass book introduces the history behind a particular collectible, the fascinating aspects that make it special, and exclusive tips on where and how to search for exciting pieces.

Furthermore, the Collector's Compass series is uniquely reliable. Each volume is created by a carefully chosen team of dealers, appraisers, collectors, and other experts. Their collaboration ensures that each title will contain accurate and current information, as well as the secrets they've learned in a lifetime of collecting.

We hope that in the Collector's Compass series we have addressed every area essential to building a collection. Whether you're a newcomer or an experienced collector, we're sure this series will lead you to new treasures. Enjoy the adventure!

WHY COLLECT '60s AND '70s DECOR?

The Appeal of '60s and '70s Decor

Many people count themselves lucky to have grown up in the turbulent '60s and the psychedelic '70s. The decades of Camelot and the Great Society were characterized by an unbridled optimism the likes of which we haven't seen since. America was infatuated with the possibilities of automation; we fantasized about how domestic robots were about to turn household drudgery into newfound leisure time. And whether we were listening to the instrumental hit "Telstar" on our new miniature transistorized radios or watching *The Outer Limits* on TV, we couldn't help thinking about the brave new world of our future in space.

Eventually, this upbeat mood came to be mirrored in the international design community. In the years leading up to 1960, the American companies that had been at the forefront of mid-century modern design moved away from home furnishings and into the corporate contract furnishings market, where they saw higher profits. At the same time, the proliferation of cheap '50s knockoff furniture was wearing out the style's welcome with American consumers, who were, perhaps grudgingly, trading in their "trendy" modern designs for tired but established styles like American colonial.

Opposite: Anna Castelli Ferrieri 4955 and 4966 modular units (popularly referred to as "Round-Ups") for Kartell (Italy), 1969. *Photo courtesy of designaddict.com.*

In short, the design world was ripe for a change. And that's precisely what it got, thanks to a corps of talented European industrial designers (notably in Italy) who were able to exploit new production techniques to create exciting designs from a seemingly mundane material—plastic. Suddenly it was possible to injection-mold ABS plastic into fun but functional shapes that were in perfect step with the freewheeling times (would you believe chairs shaped like giant molars or huge pieces of candy?). When reinvented in plastic, things as banal as storage drawers took center stage in screaming pop colors like lime green and tangerine orange. And befitting the space-age programming they delivered, even our radios and TVs took on the futuristic shapes of space stations and flying saucers.

Is it any wonder that collectors of '60s and '70s decor often trace their love of the field to feelings of nostalgia? Now perhaps in their thirties and forties, these collectors may look back with a desire to recapture their childhood. Indeed, as each generation moves into adulthood (and the resulting mix of responsibility and financial independence), it initiates a popular revival of cultural representations of its childhood. Today, for example, we can relive the '60s at the movies (the *Austin Powers* series) and in auto showrooms (the new Volkswagen Beetle); the '70s live again on the small screen (*That '70s Show*) and on the radio (the resurgence of disco music).

But perhaps more important than mere nostalgia, '60s and '70s decor offers abundant opportunities for collectors to make a statement about themselves—including their connection to society as a whole. The person who collects "happy face" memorabilia is saying something different than someone who collects so-called documented design. But both are making a statement about their place in society and the memories, attitudes, or values that are important to them.

Best of all, '60s and '70s decor satisfies the collecting bug simply because of its appealing balance between scarcity and availability. Because most products of the era were mass-produced, enough items are still available to attract the beginning collector. And the rarer "connoisseur" pieces—some produced and sold mainly in

Europe—keep seasoned collectors interested. It doesn't take long for new collectors to amass enough pieces to create an entire themed display room, if they so desire. In fact, more than one collector has taken the next step and eventually decorated the entire house in a '60s or '70s theme.

Where to Find '60s and '70s Decor

As in any field of collecting, where you should look depends almost entirely on what you are trying to find. For example, although it's possible to spot the occasional Kartell plastic storage unit at a consignment shop or neighborhood garage sale, the likelihood of finding high-style designer items at these venues is small. Your best bet for locating such pieces, albeit not at flea-market prices, is a metropolitan shop that specializes in mid-century furnishings and collectibles. That said, following are some options for refining your search.

Anna Castelli Ferrieri 4970 modular units for Kartell (Italy), 1967. *Photo courtesy of designaddict.com.*

- **Garage sales, rummage sales, and tag sales.** These are great places for finding domestically produced objects or designs, especially fashions and kitchenware, that originally were targeted to mainstream American consumers. Bargains can be had, as many sellers don't realize they have something collectible.
- **Estate sales and auctions.** If there is a preview period before the sale or auction, by all means take a look, but be aware that most of these venues rarely anticipate any interest in "that '60s junk" and will not bother to offer it.
- **Organized flea markets.** These are great sources for collectibles of this era; flea markets in metropolitan areas are particularly

worthwhile. You can expect to pay a little more than you would at a garage sale or tag sale, but your odds of finding something good are much better. Generally, sellers at flea markets go to garage and tag sales and buy up what they think they can resell. These folks, called pickers, usually know a little bit about everything and have developed a good eye for quality pieces.

- **General or specialized dealers.** When you are looking for rarities and pieces that are more difficult to find, start your search here. Mainstream antiques shops are just beginning to stock items from this period. Expect to pay a premium price for the one-stop-shopping convenience, though. Beginning collectors can usually glean a wealth of information from browsing at these shops and talking to the dealers.
- **Antiques-and-collectibles shows.** If you live in or around a major metropolitan area, you probably have access to at least one of these shows during the course of a year. Ask dealers in your area what shows they participate in. Aside from the chance of making a good find, you will have the opportunity to form a network with collectors in your area and dealers from across the country.
- **Online auctions.** Online auction sites such as eBay have become a key resource for '60s and '70s collectors—so much so that we'll go into detail about them in a later chapter. Collecting '60s and '70s decor is still such a young field that many online sellers do not realize the value of what they are selling.
- **Live auctions.** In recent years, there's been a proliferation of twentieth-century-design auctions—from the big, general houses such as Sotheby's, Christie's, and Philips to specialty houses such as Treadway and L.A. Modern. Out-of-towners can usually bid by mail or telephone.
- **Web sites.** The Internet is the perfect vehicle for small specialty businesses, and '60s and '70s collecting is no exception. There are now dozens of Web sites that offer period objects. Many are based in Europe, where the supply of some types of pieces is more plentiful.

Verner Panton's Flower Pot hanging lamp for Louis Poulsen (Denmark), 1967. *Photo courtesy of designaddict.com.*

Ways to Collect and Organize '60s and '70s Decor

Collectors of '60s and '70s decor seem to share an interest in an especially wide range of objects and a wide range of designers and manufacturers. Still, there are those who prefer to collect according to a particular niche or theme. Here are some of the most popular.

- **By designer.** Collectors may gravitate toward a specific designer or group of designers of the period. For example, they may have been won over early by the bold geometric designs of Verner Panton or the modular, minimalist look of pieces by Joe Colombo.
- **By theme.** Space-age-style electronics are some of the most popular collectibles of the period, and some collectors are so enamored of them that they look no further.
- **By pattern or color.** Especially for collectors who enjoy living with their pieces in a dedicated room or whole-house setting, collecting coordinated furnishings of a particular color is a popular pursuit. Likewise, dinnerware collectors may want to amass a collection of a particular pattern.

As a beginning collector, don't be concerned if you can't immediately identify a particular niche that appeals to you. It may take several years of collecting and learning to fine-tune your taste. Even then, you may prefer to take a larger view of modernism as a whole with your collection, cherry-picking pieces from a spectrum of styles, designers, and themes. That's part of the fun of collecting '60s and '70s decor—there's something here for everyone and there's no right or wrong way to proceed.

Does Size Really Matter?

Just one word of caution. Many collectors find that '60s and '70s decor is not easy to mix and match with other decorating styles. Although it's possible, for example, to group smaller items like period electronics on a display shelf and let them live happily alongside pieces from other styles, it's a bit more problematic with larger pieces like furniture and lighting.

That's one reason why many collectors choose to decorate whole rooms and sometimes entire homes with '60s and '70s collectibles—and, often, accumulate huge collections. Even individuals who are lucky enough to have the room and budget to acquire such "to die for" collections generally agree that, in the end, it is quality and not quantity that really matters.

Values and Trends

As someone who's just starting out in a new field of collecting, you no doubt have many questions about everything from what you can expect to pay for pieces to what they may be worth years from now. (You may even be a bit curious about whether you fit the "typical profile" of the '60s and '70s collector.) Although no one can predict with certainty the values and trends in any field of collecting, experienced collectors of '60s and '70s decor offer the following advice.

What's the investment potential?

Get ready for some good news: Values have steadily risen in this field, most notably in the area of electronics. Pieces that had only nominal value just a decade ago now command substantial prices. In some cases, values have increased as much as 500 to 700 percent in as few as five years.

That said, please don't make the mistake of assuming that any item you buy from the '60s or '70s is bound to appreciate. After all, the main reason to collect in the first place should be that you love the pieces, not to turn a fast buck.

How long have people collected '60s and '70s decor?

Relative to almost all other areas of collecting, not long at all. And that's part of why the field is currently so hot. (When design icons of the era start showing up in commercials and music videos, you can be sure something's up!) Suddenly, it seems, pieces from the '60s and '70s have achieved a newfound respectability. There now are a number of good academic design books available to help collectors research the field—there have also been recent museum exhibitions. Today, it's not unusual to see rare Joe Colombo designs offered alongside Tiffany lamps and Art Deco furnishings in twentieth-century-design auctions.

Does that mean there is a healthy market for '60s and '70s collectibles?

Most definitely! For proof, just log on to eBay. You will find a steady stream of new collectors and seasoned pros in intense bidding for the choicest examples from the era. And for the rarest pieces, there are new record prices being set at auctions as collectors and museums vie for prime examples of '60s and '70s design classics. For example, a Joe Colombo Tube chair recently brought a record $8,625; an Ettore Sottsass Asteroid lamp sold for about $6,400.

Great, but what's out there for new collectors who are on a budget?

Fortunately, there's plenty, and the collector who's just starting out is in an enviable position. You can find Massimo Vignelli plastic tableware for $5 a piece—or even less. Vintage Kartell furnishings in good condition can be had for under $200 (although you may pay a bit of a premium for the most desirable colors, such as orange, green, and yellow). If your taste runs to electronics, you will find original Panasonic radios for as little as $25. Even examples of period European lighting not originally sold in the U.S. are within reach of the beginning collector, thanks to the price-leveling effect of global bidding on Internet auction sites such as eBay.

Modular pencil holder, Geometrix (Great Britain). *Photo courtesy of designaddict.com.*

Are there certain "overheated" areas of '60s and '70s decor that I should avoid?

Not really. In recent years, there has been a steep rise in the value of some '60s and '70s pieces, especially electronics, but even prices in that segment seem to have stabilized. Currently, the items that tend to command the highest prices are rare examples by the major designers of the period (Joe Colombo, Verner Panton, and Pierre Paulin) and early works by designers who would go on to influence design in the following decades (Ettore Sottsass, Gaetano Pesce, and Frank Gehry).

But does the market for '60s and '70s collectibles still offer opportunities to buy low and sell high?

There will still be magic moments when you spot and snatch up an out-and-out bargain, and they usually occur when you happen to know more about an item than the person who is selling it. That's why knowledge of the field is so important. You are already taking the first step toward finding your own bargains just by reading this book.

Are '60s and '70s collectibles likely to appreciate further?

In such a new field, the chances are very good that the highest-quality items in the best condition will always prove to be good investments. If the long-term value of your pieces is important to you—and for some who collect solely from the heart instead of the pocketbook, it isn't—then you'll probably be best served by seeking out only the quintessential or rare examples by the most noteworthy designers and manufacturers of the period.

What's the "typical profile" of someone who collects '60s and '70s decor?

That's a tough one! Collectors of this period range from twenty-somethings who buy their pieces at the shops of trendy specialty dealers to folks in their forties who may be living with a houseful of original pieces they've accumulated since they were in their teens. One thing we can generalize about, however (even if we can't explain the phenomenon): the vast majority of '60s and '70s buffs are men.

The Bargains Really Are in "the Basement"

As with most fields of collecting, you are less likely to come across an underpriced gem in the showroom of a specialty dealer than you are somewhere a bit lower on the food chain, such as a garage sale or flea market. That's because dealers are professionals whose living depends on knowing the true value of the pieces they sell. The sellers at garage sales and flea markets may have little or no clue about what they have. One collector we know bought a rare Eero Aarnio dining-room set at a flea market for $300 and sold it later that day for $1,200. He says he could have gotten more if he had waited, but he did not have room for the pieces in his small living room.

Collecting Kitsch: When It's So Bad, It's Good

"Kitsch" is a German word that crossed over into English in the 1920s which means—loosely—"trash." Applied to '60s and '70s design, it refers to items that are of low quality and/or negligible design merit—things well outside the realm of "documented design."

Kitsch decor and accessories drew inspiration from comics and cartoons, movies and pop music—in general, the most expendable and pedestrian aspects of materialism and mass-market consumer culture. The lurid colors, unnaturally juxtaposed elements, and exaggerated ornamentation of many examples packed a shock-value punch that worked in the moment. Once the joke was over, though, the impact dissipated, and so did interest in the piece itself.

Die-hard kitsch collectors, though, remained steadfast in their support. For those who are irresistibly drawn to '60s and '70s kitsch, the more bizarre, garish, and self-parodying the object, the better. The lower the taste level, the stronger the appeal. For some, pop-culture artifacts—everything from peace-symbol buttons and jewelry to "happy face" glassware and daisy canister sets—fill the bill. Others are drawn to space-age electronics from the '70s, such as Panasonic's colorful and funky Toot-a-Loop bracelet radios.

"Happy face" wastebasket. *Photo courtesy of Fremont Antique Mall.*

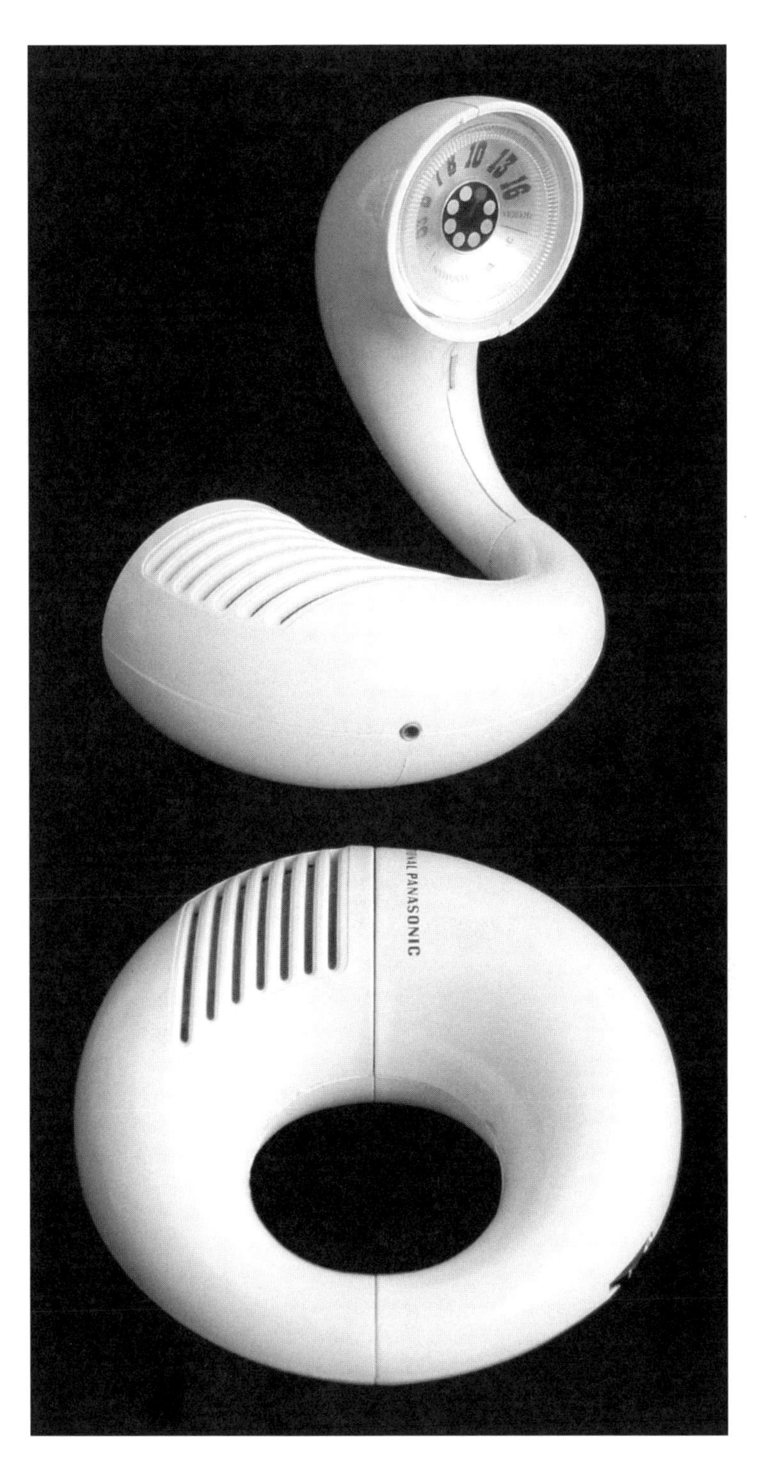

Toot-a-Loop bracelet radio, Panasonic (Japan), designed in 1972. *Photo courtesy of designaddict.com.*

Electrohome (Canada) Tabletop Smartie record player, smoked acrylic and aluminum, 1970. *Photos courtesy of Fremont Antique Mall.*

ESSENTIAL BACKGROUND ON '60s AND '70s DECOR

The Origins of '60s and '70s Design

By the end of the Second World War, the industrial infrastructures of most European nations had been devastated. It would take a decade and a half to recover, but by 1960, Europe—in particular, Italy—had begun to make great strides in industrial design and production. With its long tradition in the successful marriage of art and industry, Italy established itself as the center of new design.

Here at home, the vibrant young president Kennedy vowed that the U.S. would put a man on the moon by the decade's end, thus beginning the "race to space." As if on cue, it wasn't long before products inspired by the fantasy and technology of space travel began to appear in the marketplace. The success of pop art, with its giant versions of banal household objects, and op art, with its bold colors and dizzying optical patterns, was also mirrored in consumer products of the day.

In both Italy and the United States, the material of choice for these consumer products seemed to come out of left field: plastic, previously used only to imitate other materials, finally came into its own. Glossy injection-molded ABS, rigid fiberglass, expandable foam, and slick vinyl were the materials of the brave new world of the Jetsons. Plastics, and the new manufacturing technologies for their production, freed designers from the archetypal forms of the past and allowed them to create designs without historic precedent.

Collecting Space-Age Electronics

The year was 1969. Neil Armstrong walked on the moon, and suddenly every American kid wanted to be an astronaut. This turn of events was not lost on the marketers of consumer electronics. Soon Japanese electronics companies such as JVC and Panasonic were flooding the market with radical new designs that captured in bright-colored plastic America's preoccupation with space. Walking a fine line between legitimate design and throwaway kitsch, these head-turning televisions and radios struck a responsive chord with American consumers.

In 1970, JVC introduced its Videosphere portable TV, whose rounded plastic case was the very antithesis of the way televisions were "supposed" to look. Panasonic followed a couple of years later with its elongated spherical "flying saucer" set, complete with tripod pedestal legs and rear-mounted antennae.

Perhaps realizing that the real money to be made was with the youth market, Panasonic introduced two futuristic radio designs, both variations on the doughnut shape and executed in the bright pop colors of the day. The Toot-a-Loop radio could be worn as a bracelet; the companion Panapet radio has been called the electronic equivalent of the pet rock. Both were huge market successes.

On July 20, 1969, people the world over reacted with awe and delight as Neil Armstrong and Buzz Aldrin set foot on the moon. *Apollo 11*'s success contributed to a giddy optimism, and industrial designers responded with futuristic shapes and space-related themes. *Photo courtesy of NASA.*

The Videosphere from JVC (Japan, ca. 1970) was consciously designed to resemble an astronaut's helmet. Two versions of the base exist: the simple version illustrated here and another with an integrated clock-radio. *Photo courtesy of Erica George Dines.*

Manufacturers: The Dynamic Duo

Although '60s and '70s design was exemplified by dozens of (mostly European) manufacturers such as Heller, Bernini, Olivetti, and Danese, there are two Italian firms whose names have become synonymous with the period.

Kartell was founded in 1950, initially to manufacture small plastic household items. Through innovation, experimentation, and investment in new technology, the company developed manufacturing techniques that enabled it to produce large furnishings using injection-molded plastics. Kartell also produced lighting and household goods. The company pioneered a system of working with various designers on a freelance basis, allowing it to build a collection of products by a stellar roster that included Joe Colombo, Gino Colombini, Franco Raggi, Anna Castelli Ferrieri, Achille and Pier Giacomo Castiglioni, Giotto Stoppino, Marco Zanuso, Gae Aulenti, Richard Sapper, and Carlo Bartoli. Unique to the company was a system whereby plastics manufacturers around the world were licensed to produce Kartell products, eliminating the need for costly sea and overland freight. All Kartell goods are now manufactured at the company plant outside Milan.

Ernesto Gismondi founded **Artemide** in 1959 with the mission to produce modern-design lighting that embodied the qualities of form, function, innovation, and efficiency. Artemide has manufactured lighting designs by Vico Magistretti, Enzo Mari, Anna Fasolis, Angelo Mangiarotti, Gruppo Architetti Urbanisti Città Nuova, Gio Ponti, Emma Gismondi-Schweinberger, Gae Aulenti, and others. Its products are represented in every major modern design collection and have received numerous awards. Using its existing production and distribution systems, Artemide expanded into the furnishings market in 1966 with designs by Vico Magistretti, Sergio Mazza, and Emma Gismondi-Schweinberger, among others. Richard Sapper's Tizio desk lamp, first marketed in 1972, became one of Artemide's most enduringly popular designs. Today the firm continues to manufacture a wide range of lighting by an international array of designers.

Joe Colombo KD 27 lamp for Kartell (Italy), 1967. The KD 27 can be used singly or stacked to form a column of light. The version at left features a tray for storage. *Photo courtesy of designaddict.com.*

The Philosophy Behind '60s and '70s Design

The original concept behind much of '60s and '70s design was the creation of well-designed objects and furnishings that could be made widely available at low prices through technology and mass production. But in reality, production runs were rarely sizable enough to offset the costs of the manufacturing molds, so prices generally stayed high.

Many of the designs had an immediate appeal for young people. No surprise here: With the optimistic and youthful nature of the objects themselves, the young-adult market was the natural target. A great example is Olivetti's Valentine portable typewriter, designed by Ettore Sottsass in 1969. Olivetti's marketing of the Valentine took it out of the realm of office machines or even equipment for students. Instead, the typewriter was advertised being used by glamorous young models, and was placed in upscale boutiques as a "must have" fashion accessory. The Valentine's lightweight plastic case and lipstick-red color had both novelty and status appeal—in much the same way that sleek and ever-more-miniature cell phones capture the fascination of young people today. It was a huge commercial success.

Ettore Sottsass and Perry King's Valentine portable typewriter for Olivetti (Italy), 1969. The typewriter shown here is ready for use, but it can be slipped into a matching cover for easy portability. *Photo courtesy of Erica George Dines.*

Much of '60s and '70s design also embodied the three Ms: it was mobile, modular, and multi-functional. Furnishings were often mounted on casters; chairs and tables could be stacked; end tables became bookcases; furniture went from the patio to the living room; and appliances became portable. For the first time, consumers could buy a finite number of modular elements and arrange them in an infinite number of configurations with a wide range of uses.

The "Demise" of '60s and '70s Design

The United States and Europe enjoyed a mostly optimistic atmosphere during the early 1960s. This was a time of social change at almost every level of society. The civil-rights movement, the sexual revolution, the hippie counterculture, the race to space, and a prosperous economy all seemed to point toward a brighter future. However, by the end of the 1960s, society's outlook darkened. The civil-rights movement turned more volatile, the sexual revolution gave way to soaring divorce rates, the hippie counterculture deteriorated under heavy drug use, NASA suffered setbacks and loss of public interest, and the war in Vietnam divided the nation.

The OPEC oil crisis of 1973 had the most direct effect on the design industry. Petroleum was a "silent partner" in the success of space-age design—plastic being a petroleum-based product. As the price of the once-inexpensive raw material skyrocketed, manufacturing costs were pushed to previously unimaginable levels. After 1973, many of the slower-selling plastic designs were taken out of production and fewer new designs were introduced. The products that continued in manufacture reflected this attitude shift. Gone were the bright pop primary colors of the '60s; in their place were the "natural" tones of chocolate brown, avocado green, and harvest gold of the middle and late '70s.

The industrial designers of the '60s and '70s saw the potential of plastic and, by successfully utilizing its unique properties, gave the material a new dignity. Nonetheless, many consumers could not overcome their prejudices against the material. Plastic might have been fine for the patio, but it wasn't appropriate for the living room and certainly couldn't command "designer prices." Ultimately, it was the low-quality, inexpensive knockoff designs that did succeed in mass production, and to consumers used to more traditional materials, these poorly manufactured pieces only reinforced a low esteem for plastic.

By the mid-1970s, it became clear that we would not suit up in our space gear and commute to the moon anytime soon. Gone was the fascination and fantasy of space travel. But the technology generated by the space program would lead to the next chapter in modern design, as the focus shifted from the rounded curves of the space age to the hard edges of neo-formalism and high-tech.

Materials and Manufacture

Plastic—the very material we now take for granted in everything from shampoo bottles to trash bags—was anything but mundane to designers in the '60s and '70s. It was easy to mold into almost any conceivable shape, allowing designers greater freedom to create new forms. For example, a chair no longer needed to be supported by four legs. It could be formed by a single curved plane, shaped like a giant pill or huge blades of grass, or set on a central pedestal. Injection-molded ABS and sturdy fiberglass were the staples of furniture designers, but inflatable furniture, made from sheets of clear PVC and filled with air, began to be made. Foam rubber was used for simple padding as well as elaborate soft sculptures.

The Key Manufacturing Processes

Although plastic itself was not a material new to the 1960s, the processes by which it was manufactured into objects most certainly were. Firms such as Kartell were leaders in the development of high-quality precision injection molding. Previously, injection molding was used almost exclusively for small, inexpensive items; it is not uncommon to see seam lines and variations in thickness in older (or cheaply made) plastics. But with the new injection-molding techniques, manufacturers could produce chairs, tables, and desks as well as smaller objects with incredible precision and a fine fit and finish. New production methods were even developed to meet the needs of specific products.

A good example is the Cantilever chair designed by Verner Panton. Although Panton originally designed the chair in 1960, the technology to manufacture the piece commercially did not exist until 1967. The sinuous form of the single-piece chair was a completely original concept that expanded the parameters of manufacturing.

The Markings and Packaging of '60s and '70s Design

To the benefit of collectors, most examples of '60s and '70s design are easy to identify. At the very least, the name of the manufacturer will appear on the piece; often it is accompanied by the name of the designer, the country of origin, the name of the design and/or a style number, and even the date of the design or manufacture. On plastic items, the information is simply molded into the piece itself. On glass, metal, and ceramic items, it is included in some other way appropriate for the material, such as on a foil or paper label. In the increasingly name-conscious marketplace of the era, manufacturers were eager for consumers to know who they were, and designers often negotiated for their names to appear on their designs.

Some '60s and '70s designs were packaged in boxes or carriers that reflected the aesthetic of the products' designers. For example, the Lella and Massimo Vignelli stacking plastic dinnerware for Heller came in simple white-board boxes with plain orange type—a decidedly unassuming and modern approach. The Up series chair by Gaetano Pesce came vacuum-packed in PVC envelopes. When opened, the chairs self-inflated into various sculptural forms over the course of the next several hours.

How '60s and '70s Design Became Collectible

One could say that the first collectors of '60s and '70s design were museums, such as the Museum of Modern Art in New York, which solicited manufacturers for examples of objects that they considered significant at their introduction. With this endorsement, it was almost assured that private collectors of twentieth-century design would also want to include the pieces in their personal collections.

New Materials, New Uses

Plastic was not the only material to inspire furniture designers to experimental applications. In 1972 the young Frank Gehry (who would go on to become the most influential architect of the 1990s) introduced the Easy Edges line of furnishings, consisting of chairs, stools, lounges, tables, bookcases, and beds. It was unique in being made from ordinary corrugated cardboard. Although the line was a huge commercial success, Gehry decided to end production after only three months, making the original pieces much sought after today. Some of the Easy Edges pieces were reintroduced by Vitra Design Museum in 1996.

Massimo and Lella Vignelli's Max 1 melamine tableware for Heller (U.S.A.), 1964. *Photo courtesy of designaddict.com.*

Massimo Vignelli Max mug for Heller (U.S.A.), melamine, 1972. *Photo courtesy of Fremont Antique Mall.*

All Massimo Vignelli plastic tableware is marked on the underside, making identification easy. Examples produced prior to 1973 are marked "Made in Italy." *Photo courtesy of Fremont Antique Mall.*

The Early Appeal of '60s and '70s Decor

Private collectors finally did discover the period in the late 1980s to mid-1990s—they were individuals who had previously been in the forefront of collecting other modern design periods. Perhaps they had grown tired of amassing '50s designs, or maybe they were just intrigued by the unusual shapes and colors seen in many '60s pieces. These designs were unique in the canon of modernism. No wonder people discovered that they simply enjoyed owning them.

Many well-heeled collectors traveled to Europe in search of treasures at shops and flea markets. Fortunately for the rest, at about this time the Internet was emerging as a force, and Web sites selling these newly discovered collectibles began to appear. In addition, museums were assembling exhibitions that featured prominent designs of the era, and books were published that legitimized the field and exposed it to a much wider audience (see "Recommended Books" on pages 121–122).

Noteworthy Collections of '60s and '70s Design

- Museum of Modern Art, New York City
- Vitra Design Museum, Weil am Rhein and Berlin
- Cooper-Hewitt, National Design Museum, New York City
- Design Museum, London
- Plasticarium, Brussels
- Victoria and Albert Museum, London
- Montreal Museum of Decorative Arts

Before You Start Collecting

What You Need to Know About the Marketplace

As you're about to see, there's no single "marketplace" for '60s and '70s decor. Rather, the collective marketplace consists of everything from the garage sale down the street to a variety of dealer locations to high-end auctions at well-known houses such as Christie's and Treadway. And for the new collector, each marketplace sector offers its own special opportunities and has its own set of rules. Here are tips on some of the most common.

Garage Sales, Yard Sales, and Tag Sales

Depending on what area of '60s and '70s decor you're seeking, there definitely are finds to be made at the grass-roots level of garage, yard, and tag sales. Look especially for Heller dinnerware; Kartell, Artemide, and Stendig furniture; Raymor Modern ceramics; and Lightolier lamps. The suburbs around larger cities and communities where seniors retire are often prime hunting grounds. Still, be prepared to spend entire days hunting and end up with little or nothing to show for it.

Opposite: Yrjö Kukkapuro's Karuselli armchair for Haimi-Oy (Finland), 1965. *Photo courtesy of Marlon Gobel.*

COLLECTOR'S COMPASS

TM

The Golden Rules of Collecting

1. Buy Quality, Not Quantity

It's all too easy to buy many items of inconsequential value—and spend a fortune doing so. Try to buy the very best you can afford.

2. Invest in Books, Subscriptions, and Auction Catalogs

A little education will go a long way toward giving you an accurate understanding of what's truly valuable. You'll find that your reference library gets lots of use as you begin to collect.

3. Collect What You Like

No one can predict with certainty which items will increase in value over time. So it's important to enjoy the pieces you buy for what they are, not as potential investments.

4. Be Active

Networking with shop owners and fellow collectors is one of your best collecting strategies. It's important to continue growing in your knowledge about the field and to gather firsthand experiences at a variety of outlets.

5. Be Patient

You'll come to realize that more good items come along than most of us could ever hope to afford. Try to focus on the pieces you truly value or that have a great value themselves.

6. Be Fair

Take pride in conducting yourself in a respectful and generous manner. Building relationships is the key to building a great collection, and collectors reap what they sow.

7. Add to the History

Keep good records of the items you buy. Remember that you're a link in the story that each piece has to tell. Try to leave your pieces in the same—or better—condition than when you bought them.

8. Nurture Your Personal Vision

Don't let reference books dictate what you should and shouldn't collect. Collecting by rote is a lifeless pursuit. Look beyond the icons in the field, and let your creativity and personality guide your choices.

Estate Sales and Estate Auctions

Although it's certainly possible to find the occasional collectible from this period at estate sales and estate auctions, keep in mind that '60s and '70s decor wasn't an especially popular decorating style during the decades when these items were widely available. You'll increase your chances by visiting estate sales in or near urban areas, which seemed, to a greater extent than rural America, to embrace the extremes in modern design.

Flea Markets, Bazaars, and Thrift Shops

Even though it's becoming harder to find '60s and '70s items (much less bargains) at flea markets, bazaars, and thrift shops, many collectors still swear by them. The operative rule here is to visit regularly and often—the earlier in the day, the better. Find out when the dealers start to set up, and try to get there just as they arrive. If that happens to be before sunrise, take your flashlight!

Consignment Shops

If you're lucky enough to find the right consignment shops, you may well snag some desirable pieces. Those that sell used furnishings are the best bets. You'll save yourself time and disappointment by calling ahead to inquire about the merchandise a specific shop sells.

Unlike thrift shops, which receive merchandise through donations, consignment shops build inventory by paying sellers a percentage of the selling price after the item has sold. If an item hasn't sold after a specified period, it's customary for the shop to mark it down by a certain percentage. These periodic price reductions usually continue over whatever period the shop has agreed to display the item.

> *Playing "The Price Is Right"*
>
> If you frequent consignment shops, you may be tempted to let an item you like sit a little longer in order to get it at a discounted price. Sometimes this strategy works. But keep in mind that someone else may snatch it up in the meantime. Don't risk losing something you really want over a few dollars. If you'd be happy with the item at the marked price, grab it when you see it!

The Internet

One of the easiest places to find an abundance of '60s and '70s decor is on the Internet. Here's a sampling of where you'll find it.

- **eBay and other online auctions.** These are perhaps your best bet for finding bargains on the Internet.
- **Dealer Web sites.** The sites of specialized dealers, both here and abroad, are wonderful sources for building your collection. Of course, dealers' prices are likely to be at or close to market value, but the occasional bargain can be found.
- **Online classified ads.** Sites featuring items of modern design such as deco-echoes.com, gomod.com, and designaddict.com offer free classified ads, which are great places to pick up specific items from collections that are being sold off.
- **E-groups.** Subscribing to e-groups devoted to the buying and selling of '60s and '70s decor can increase your exposure to items available for sale.

Sven-Eric Juhlin's record holder for Gustavsberg (Sweden), 1970s. *Photo courtesy of Area 51.*

Antiques-and-Collectibles Malls

Antiques-and-collectibles malls are composed of booths rented to individual sellers, usually on a monthly basis. A single mall may have forty or more booths. With so many individual sellers, the type and quality of the merchandise for sale varies widely. If you don't mind looking at many items you have little or no interest in, shopping here may be your cup of tea. As a reward for time and patience, it's common for buyers to ask for (and get) a better price on purchases at malls.

Specialty Shops

New shops that specialize in '60s and '70s decor spring up all the time, although shops that deal more generally in postwar design are still more common. You'll find ads and listings for both in magazines such as *Echoes* and *The Modernism Magazine.* These ads are especially helpful in locating dealers in cities you'll be visiting. Even if you're not on a buying expedition, such visits will give you the opportunity to compare prices in different parts of the country, make new contacts, and meet fellow collectors and dealers.

ART CENTER COLLEGE OF DESIGN LIBRARY

Join the Virtual '60s and '70s Collecting Community

Before the Internet, there were few opportunities for collectors of '60s and '70s decor to exchange information. But now there are numerous modernism Web sites that provide links to individual dealers' sites. Many of these so-called aggregation sites offer community areas where visitors can share information. In essence, these message boards and discussion groups serve the same purpose as the collectors' clubs of the past—but with the added advantage of unlimited geographic reach.

On the Internet, visitors can share tips on their favorite sources and shops, the care and restoration of their prized pieces, and dates of upcoming sales and events. This is also where some members first offer pieces for sale—giving regular participants the first opportunity to buy items that may be highly prized.

Antiques-and-Collectibles Shows

Shows are a great way to meet dealers and fellow collectors, purchase reference books and items for your collection, and just marvel at all the pieces for sale. The rule of thumb for shows is: The more specialized the show, the better the merchandise, the greater the selection, and the higher the prices.

Seasoned collectors will tell you that the best way to "walk a show" is early and quickly! If you have the benefit of attending with someone else, split up and cover different areas simultaneously. With a pair of walkie-talkies or cell phones, it's just like having another pair of eyes. After your initial run-through, make a second pass at a leisurely pace for a more thorough look, to chat with dealers, and to take notes on specific items and their prices. If you still happen to be shopping at the end of the show, this can be a great time to find bargains—sometimes dealers would rather sell an item at a slightly discounted price than pack it up and cart it home.

Auctions

Major houses such as Sotheby's, Christie's, and Philips all host design auctions; call the nearest local branch to find out about upcoming events. Even if you're not yet comfortable bidding at major auctions, attending one will give you valuable experience and information, especially if you purchase the catalog and mark down the prices realized (or request a list after the auction;

increasingly, auction houses post results on their Web sites, too). Your records will serve as reference points to current values paid in competitive situations. They'll be good reminders, or even bargaining points, when you see comparable items in shops or online auctions.

Dealing with Dealers

Dealers are such an important source for collectors—for valuable information as well as for collectible pieces themselves—that it pays to know the ins and outs of working with them. Cultivating relationships with your dealer network will pay big dividends in building a quality collection.

Do dealers know everything about what they're selling and what it's worth?

No dealer can be expected to know everything about everything. In fact, it's good that they don't—the occasions when you happen to know more about an item than the dealer who's selling it are when you'll snag real bargains.

Dealer knowledge varies widely. Savvy collectors ask their dealers questions—lots of them. When you do that, you'll soon get a sense of whether the dealer knows what he or she is talking about. That said, it rarely pays to call attention to a dealer's error—even when you know you're right. Always remain polite and nonargumentative. Listen to everything the dealer says, and then evaluate the truth and logic of what you hear.

Are most dealers honest?

Fortunately, yes. Dealers who habitually lie to their customers don't stay in business long. But as we just said, that doesn't let you off the hook for doing your homework and asking many questions. Dealers aren't out to cheat people, but they aren't always as careful as they might be, either.

As a new collector, you'll rarely go wrong if you stick with dealers who've built solid reputations. Ask around. And never enter into any major purchase ($500 or more) without some sort of written guarantee that also notes all pertinent facts about the item. A dealer who's unwilling to accommodate you on this doesn't deserve your business.

How can dealers help me build my collection?

Probably in more ways than you can imagine. First, most dealers love to talk about their merchandise and, in so doing, will give you invaluable insights and information.

Second, by building a long-term relationship with a dealer you like—by being an active collector who makes regular purchases from the dealer—you'll earn a spot on the dealer's A-list. You'll be among the first called when special items appear on the market.

I've heard that some collectors buy pieces from dealers "on approval." What does that mean?

Glad you asked. That's yet another way dealers can help you fine-tune your collection.

After you've established a solid relationship with a particular dealer, it's not uncommon for the dealer to let you take home a piece you're especially interested in to see if it really works in the context of your collection. Typically, you and the dealer will work out the price and terms of payment in advance; of course, you shouldn't ask the dealer to negotiate on price after you've taken delivery of the item.

Are dealers' prices ever negotiable?

Certainly. Never be afraid to bargain—it's part of the fun of collecting. In fact, most dealers factor in a certain amount of "wiggle room" in their asking price—anywhere from 10 to 20 percent.

Just be sure to keep your negotiations positive. Refrain from pointing out flaws or otherwise

> COLLECTOR'S COMPASS™
>
> *Want-List Wonders*
>
> An up-to-date want list in the hands of a dealer who knows you is one of the best ways to find the pieces you truly want. Leaving a want list in no way obligates you to buy a particular item, but it does show the dealer that you're serious.
>
> To make the most of your dealer network, you should be willing to pay somewhere within the range of market prices for the items on your want list. This doesn't necessarily mean top dollar, but you'll find that dealers seldom call collectors who are looking only for "wholesale-price steals."

insulting the merchandise. If a piece seems expensive, ask the dealer how he arrived at the price. Or you might say something like, "Would you be open to an offer on this piece?" or "Is there any room on the price?" If you'll be paying cash, now's the time to mention it. This sometimes works to your advantage when you're negotiating.

Take your time, but if you and the dealer eventually reach common ground in your price negotiations, by all means, be prepared to buy. To a dealer, there are few things worse than customers who negotiate as a game and really have no intention of buying.

"I'll Take It!"

A word to the wise: On those supremely memorable occasions when you happen across a sought-after item that's ridiculously underpriced, simply say "I'll take it!"

Don't discuss. Don't negotiate. Just buy it and walk away. The dealer will almost certainly eventually realize his or her mistake. And although it's fair to buy a bargain, don't add insult to injury by asking for a discount.

Is it a good idea to leave a "standing bid" with a dealer for a particular piece?

A standing bid—the highest price you're willing to pay for a piece—actually could end up working against you. That's because dealers can use it to "shop the piece around" for slightly more money. Your offer will be more compelling when it has immediacy: Say "I'll buy this piece right now for this price." Of course, that doesn't mean you wouldn't also buy it later for the same price, but such a statement might prompt the dealer to act.

Should I request a receipt for every purchase?

Yes, definitely. And it's best if the receipt includes the dealer's name and address, your name, and a description of the piece (including its approximate age and its condition). The exceptions: garage sales and flea markets, where some vendors may not give receipts; at these venues, simply record the details of your purchase in a notebook.

What if I'm not satisfied with my purchase?
Most dealers will accept merchandise for refund if it's returned in the same condition. But you should always ask about a dealer's return policy before you buy, and getting a receipt that describes the item is your first line of defense. Then if you discover that the piece isn't authentic, you have something in writing to back up your claim. Whenever you buy a high-ticket item, you should ask for a written guarantee as additional protection.

Condition is another matter, however. Carefully inspect the piece before you agree to buy it, and specifically ask the dealer questions about its condition, the originality of all pieces, and any history of repair, refinishing, or restoration.

Andy Warhol achieved notoriety when he exhibited his first Campbell's soup paintings in 1962. A striking departure from the abstract expressionism of the 1950s, pop art's depiction of everyday objects was meant to reflect the emptiness of consumer culture and underline the artist's detatchment from his work. In the '60s, some considered pop art ridiculous and ugly, while others championed it as a legitimate, easily accessible art form. The 1969 silk screen shown here, *Old Fashioned Vegetable* from Warhol's Campbell's Soup II series, sold for $3,750 at a 2000 Wright auction. *Photo courtesy of Wright.*

Participating in Online Auctions

What are the pros and cons of buying in an online auction?

Online auctions have provided greater access to collectibles than has ever existed. They've leveled the playing field, giving people in all areas of the country—and around the world—equal opportunity to sell and bid on items.

The vast majority of online auction transactions turn out well for both buyer and seller. But the downside of online auctions is that you're bidding without being able to examine the piece. If you're unsure—especially on a high-ticket item—don't hesitate to inquire about the item's condition or even request additional photos. And it never hurts to ask for a guarantee that you'll be able to return the piece for a full refund if it's not in the condition advertised.

Where can I find online auctions?

eBay, www.ebay.com, is the most popular auction site on the Internet. Amazon.com and Yahoo Auctions are two other rapidly growing sites. Shopgoodwill.com showcases items from Goodwill Thrift Shops around the country. By visiting a popular search engine and entering "online auction" as your search term, you'll generate a long list of other sites to check out, too.

How do I register for an online auction?

On eBay, one of the first headings you'll see on the home page is for a "New User" section. This explains the details of bidding and selling, both of which require you to register (you must have an e-mail address). Access the registration page, and enter your personal information. You'll find the eBay registration page at: http://pages.ebay.com/services/registration/register.html.

In order to sell items, you have to place a credit-card number on file. There's usually a small fee for placing an item on auction, and a commission when the item sells. These charges are made directly to your credit-card account and are summarized on monthly statements you'll receive from the auction site.

How do I search for the items I'm interested in?

Try searching first under the most common terms you can think of for your collectible of interest (verner panton, eero aarnio, joe colombo, artemide, pierre paulin, Italian plastic, sixties design, seventies design, 60's, 60s, 70's, 70s, op art, pop art, jvc videosphere, panapet, weltron). Savvy searchers also come up with less obvious terms that may produce misnamed or incompletely identified items (plastic shelving, plastic chair, geometric rug, futuristic, unusual, groovy, funky).

What's the best strategy for bidding in an online auction?

Although some bidders like to open with the highest price they're willing to pay (to discourage others from bidding), many bidders prefer to wait until the last possible moment before the auction's close to place their bid. This practice, called sniping, is considered unfair by some because it may not allow an item to reach its true price potential. Many new auction sites prevent sniping by automatically extending the auction deadline if a bid comes in at the last minute.

What are seller reserve prices?

The reserve price is the lowest amount that the seller is willing to accept for an item. This amount isn't disclosed (unless the seller chooses to reveal it), but if the item reaches its reserve price the listing will indicate that the reserve is met, and the item will be sold. It's considered inappropriate to e-mail a seller to ask what the reserve price is.

How does the transaction take place if I make a winning bid?

If you've placed the winning bid on an item, you'll see your user name listed as the winning bidder on the item's page. The site will then notify both you and the seller and provide your e-mail addresses. Often, the seller will send the successful bidder a note of congratulation and explain shipping and payment options. (Remember never to send a credit-card number in an e-mail.) Once you've received the item, it's customary to notify the seller that it was received in good condition.

But what if the item arrives and it isn't as described?

In that case, the seller should let you return it and refund your money. But if the item was correctly described and you're simply unhappy with it, you're probably stuck with it.

When the transaction is complete, each party should "post feedback" into the other party's profile. For example, if you made prompt payment and conducted yourself in a proper manner, the seller should

Collecting Kitsch: Learning to Love the LAVA Lamp

Even though it made its debut in 1963, the Astro lamp (as it was originally christened) actually was a full ten years in the making. Its British inventor, Edward Craven Walker, was fascinated by a wartime-vintage egg timer he discovered in a pub and was determined to turn the design into a lamp. The resulting prototype used a combination of water, wax, and a "secret formula" to produce perpetually undulating shapes.

As anyone who's ever sat transfixed by those shapes soon figures out, the lamp operates on basic principles of physics. As a low-wattage lightbulb in the base of the lamp heats the "blobs" in the elongated glass enclosure above, they become lighter and rise to

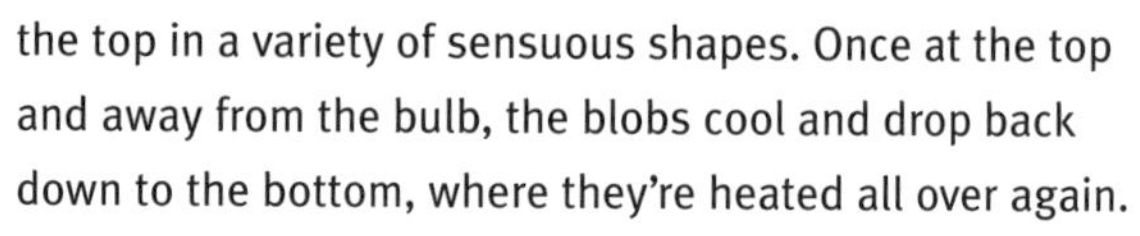

the top in a variety of sensuous shapes. Once at the top and away from the bulb, the blobs cool and drop back down to the bottom, where they're heated all over again.

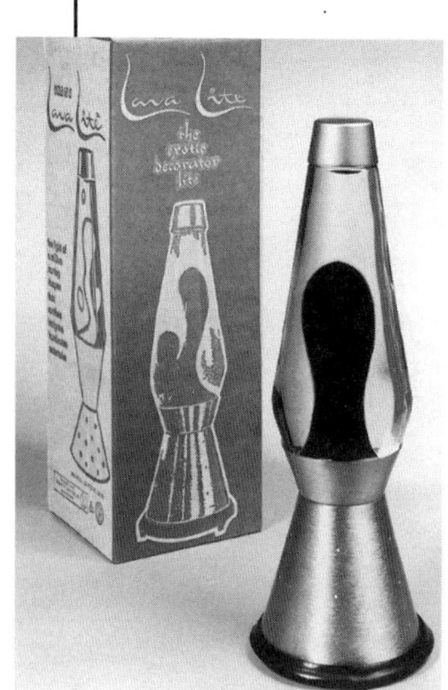

Photo courtesy of Haggerty Enterprises, Inc.

Two years after the Astro lamp's introduction in Britain, a pair of American entrepreneurs saw it exhibited at a German trade show and immediately negotiated to purchase the rights to manufacture and sell it in North America. The Chicago-based company Haggerty Enterprises soon introduced the Century model, with its signature gold base (with "starlight" holes) and your choice of red or white blobs in yellow or blue liquid. Oh, and it also renamed its creation the LAVA motion lamp.

As befits the icon of a generation that it was to become, the Century model remains in production to this day, although dozens of models have come and gone in the intervening years (including the Mediterranean, a Spanish-inspired wrought-iron lamp, and the Enchantress Planter, a lamp that bloomed with "delicate [plastic] foliage and exquisite floral greenery"). To see photos of these and other models, visit the company's entertaining Web site at www.lavaworld.com.

And the lamp collectibles just keep on coming. In the U.K., original manufacturer Mathmos has introduced the rocket-ship-shaped special-edition Telstar lamp to commemorate the new millennium. And here on these shores, Haggerty Enterprises is celebrating the lamp's longevity with a special thirty-fifth-anniversary collector's edition and a limited run of the largest LAVA-brand motion lamp ever made, weighing in at 100 pounds, standing four feet tall, and holding a full ten gallons of "secret formula." Far out!

give you positive feedback. If the seller shipped the item promptly, packaged it sufficiently, and worked to resolve any disputes, then it's customary to give the seller positive feedback. Negative feedback is a last-resort measure reserved for instances in which all methods to resolve a dispute have been tried to no avail.

Participating in Live Auctions

What are the pros and cons of buying at a live auction?

In today's market, some of the best pieces are sold at auctions that take place before a live audience. But competition can be fierce, as evidenced by the astronomical prices sometimes seen. But just as every auction has items that sell for far too much, every auction also has its share of outright bargains. Be prepared and patient, and you'll find those bargains!

How do I find out about live auctions?

Live auctions range from local countryside events attended primarily by friends and neighbors to large auctions in urban centers where museum curators, collectors, and interested parties from around the world may converge. Local newspapers also list auctions in their classifieds sections.

What's the role of the auctioneer and his crew?

The auctioneer is the person who actually takes bids for the items. He or she will pick up or point to the item up for bid and briefly describe it. Auctioneers are usually paid a commission based on the final selling price, so it's to their advantage to get the highest possible price for the items.

How should I prepare for a live auction?

Try to inspect any items you're interested in firsthand before the auction begins. Many auction houses schedule preview periods, sometimes the day before or early on the morning of the auction. This is especially crucial for expensive or rare pieces and at smaller houses that don't guarantee sales. If you can't look at an item in person, request a detailed written condition report for it. Don't assume that an object must be in good condition just because a "legitimate" auction house is offering it.

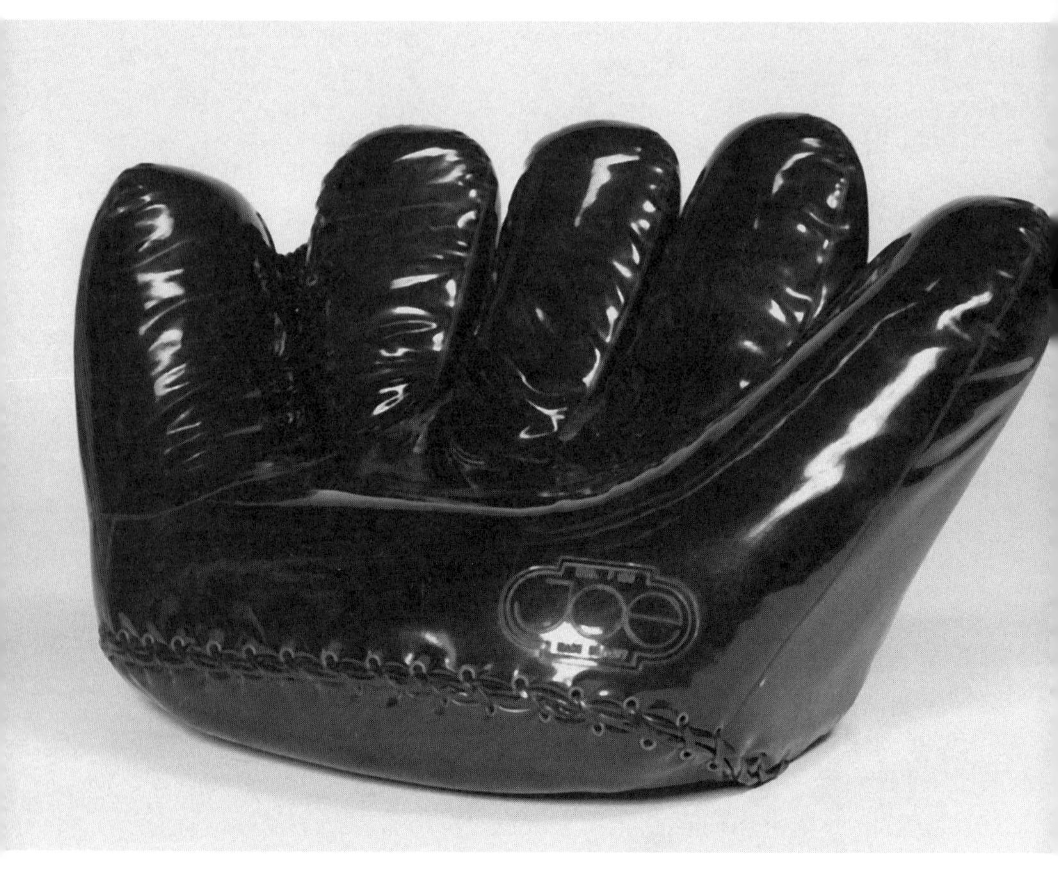

Gionatan De Pas, Donato D'Urbino, and Paolo Lomazzi "Joe" chair for Poltronova (Italy), 1970. A tongue-in-cheek tribute to Joe DiMaggio, the "glove" also made reference to the pop-art soft sculptures of Claes Oldenburg. It is made of vinyl upholstery over polyurethane foam and is "autographed" with a large label on the front. *Photo courtesy of Wright.*

Decide beforehand what you're willing to bid. This will help you avoid paying more than the item's true market value. At the same time, try to be aware of what those around you are bidding. For example, if a dealer you know across the room is still bidding, there's a good chance that the lot hasn't yet reached its true value, since the dealer probably is buying it for resale. Indeed, if you're bidding against a dealer, your chances of winning are improved, as your maximum is likely to be closer to the retail value than the wholesale value at which the dealer will likely stop bidding.

In arriving at the maximum price you'll pay, be sure to factor in any state sales tax and buyer's premium that may apply. Buyer's premiums are commissions the auctioneer charges to the winning bidders (in addition to the commissions he receives from the items' owners). Be sure to determine when you register to bid whether a buyer's premium will be charged. If the object will have to be shipped, get a shipping quote. Auction houses often have exclusive agreements with shippers that can add substantially to the final cost of the object.

Is it difficult to register to bid at a live auction?

Not at all. You can probably even do it by mail. If you have a driver's license and a credit card, you're all set. Some auction houses also ask for credit references and a bank reference if you plan to pay by check. You'll be assigned a bidder number, and at the more established auction houses you'll be issued a paddle showing your number.

Exactly how does the bidding work at a live auction?

As in online auctions, some items may have reserve prices. The auctioneer will determine the opening bid based on this reserve and on any absentee bids received before the sale. Often, bidding will start at about half of the item's "low estimate." For example, if it's expected to sell for between $600 and $1,000, the auctioneer may start the bidding at around $300.

Then, as bids come in, the bid price will escalate—usually in increments corresponding to the amount. For instance, between $100 and $500, the bid may increase in increments of $10; when the bidding reaches $500, it may increase in increments of $25. Once the bidding has topped out and the auctioneer receives no further bids, he'll close, usually with the words "Fair warning; going once; going twice; sold." If you happen to be the successful bidder, you show your paddle or call out your bidder number. In the event that the bidding doesn't reach the reserve price, the auctioneer pulls the item and it is not sold (this is called a pass).

Can I still bid if I can't be present at the auction?

Yes, indeed. Of course, it's always best to bid in person. But if you can't be present, you can preregister and submit bids for all items you're interested in (your bid may have to be higher than a certain percentage of the low estimate). Once the auction is under way, the bid will be executed as if you were there.

Joe Colombo 4801 lounge chair for Kartell (Italy), 1964, lacquered plywood. The deceptively simple design of this chair, using three interlocking pieces, required two years of technical development. *Photo courtesy of Wright.*

Verner Panton's Panthella table lamp for Louis Poulsen (Denmark), 1970.
Photo courtesy of designaddict.com.

An even better strategy is to ask if you can bid by telephone, which lets you participate live in the auction. However, you should still set your maximums and go no further by phone than you would have in person. Established auction houses have several phone lines manned by staff who will call you when your desired lot comes up and then stay on the line with you during the bidding, to increase your bid as instructed.

What's involved in claiming my winnings?

You may pick up the items you win at the auction house following the auction or, in many cases, have them shipped to you. The auction house will usually have laid out the specific policies it uses to ship merchandise; by signing the agreement, you're bound to abide by those policies. Don't even think of not honoring your winning bid. When you bid, you enter a legal contract to purchase at the agreed price, and you'll be held to your agreement. In some cases, auctioneers may be willing to arrange short-term storage for a fee (determine this beforehand when you register if it's a necessity for you). But most of the time you should be prepared to remove or arrange for immediate shipping of your winnings. And remember, once the gavel drops and you've won an item, legal title transfers to you. Any damage or loss beyond that point is your responsibility—unless the auctioneer's staff damages the piece in removing it from the podium.

Designers of the '60s and '70s were quick to embrace the notion of modular design, as shown by these stackable plastic pieces. In front are Mario Bellini's Quattro Gatti tables for C&B (Italy), 1966; behind are Olaf von Bohr's 4925-4940 bookshelves for Kartell (Italy), 1969. *Photo courtesy of Erica George Dines.*

Photo Gallery

Alexander Graham Plane, commonly known as the Airplane Phone, from Northern Telecom (U.S.A.), ca. 1977. *Photo courtesy of Fremont Antique Mall.*

Studio Tetrarch's Pistillo lamp, produced by Valenti (Italy), 1969. This chromed plastic lamp, which can be mounted on a wall or placed on a table, radiates light in a favorite op-art effect. *Photo courtesy of Wright.*

Well-known for his inventive lighting designs, Vico Magistretti's genius is displayed by the sculptural lamps shown here. From left to right: Mezzachimera, Telegono, and Dalù (all 1969), for Artemide. The Arcadia table, another Magistretti design for Artemide, dates from 1966. *Photo courtesy of Erica George Dines.*

At far left is Eero Aarnio's Pastil, or Gyro, chair for Asko Oy (Finland), 1967. Giotto Stoppino's 1972 Deda, a two-piece interlocking vase for Heller (U.S.A.), sits atop a Valetto Triangolo shelf by Ambrogio Brusa for Valenti (Italy), 1971. *Photo courtesy of Erica George Dines.*

Shown here is an assembly of children's furniture. Marco Zanuso chairs for Kartell (Italy), 1965, are stacked in the background. In the foreground, Alexander Begge chairs for Casala-Werke (Germany), 1970, flank an Efebino stool by Stacy Dukes for Artemide (Italy), ca. 1969. *Photo courtesy of Erica George Dines.*

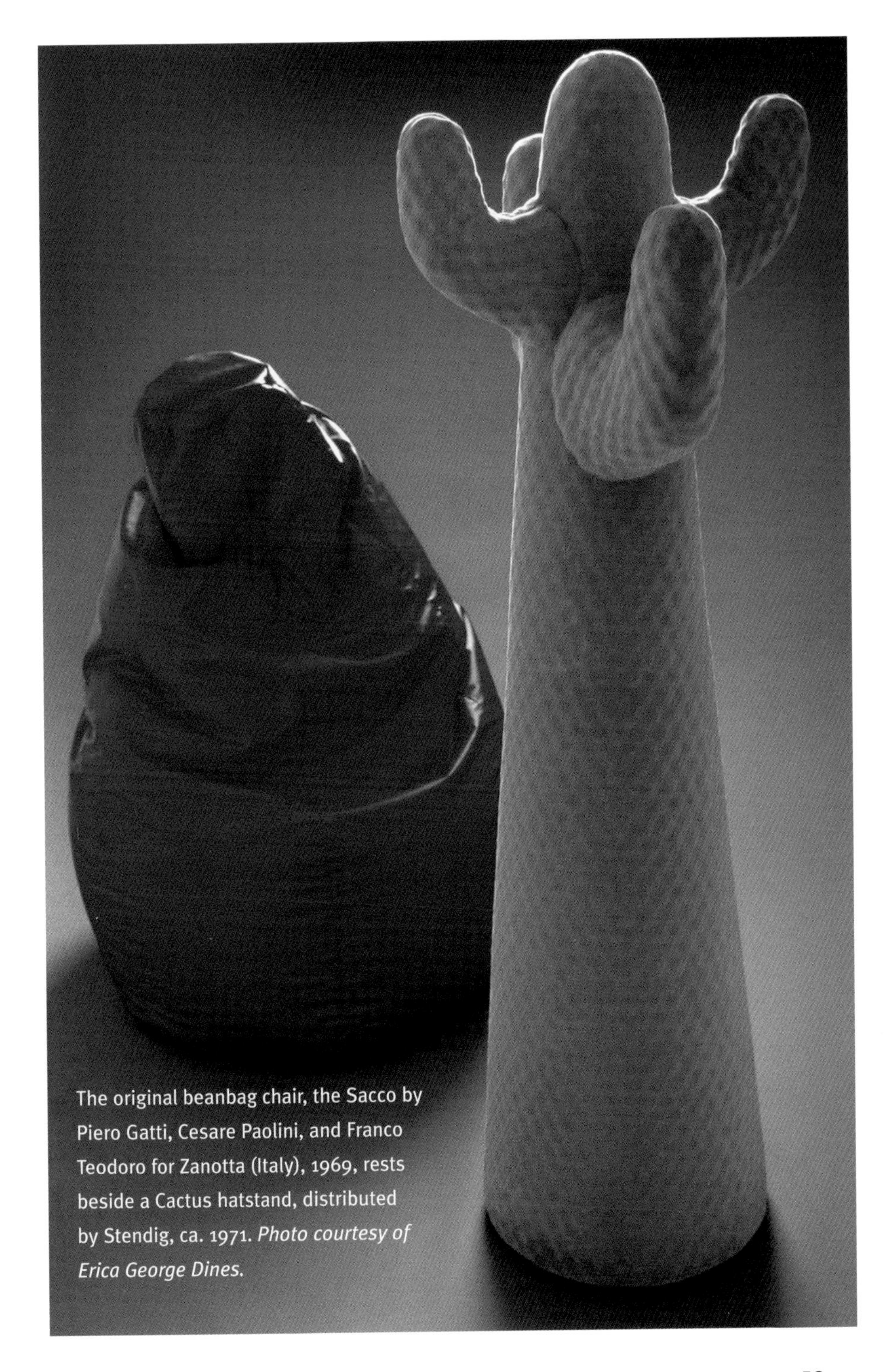

The original beanbag chair, the Sacco by Piero Gatti, Cesare Paolini, and Franco Teodoro for Zanotta (Italy), 1969, rests beside a Cactus hatstand, distributed by Stendig, ca. 1971. *Photo courtesy of Erica George Dines.*

Mario Bellini's GA 45 "Pop" automatic record player for Minerva (Italy), 1968. *Photo courtesy of designaddict.com.*

Eleonore Peduzzi Riva's Spyros ashtrays for Artemide (Italy), melamine, 1969. *Photo courtesy of designaddict.com.*

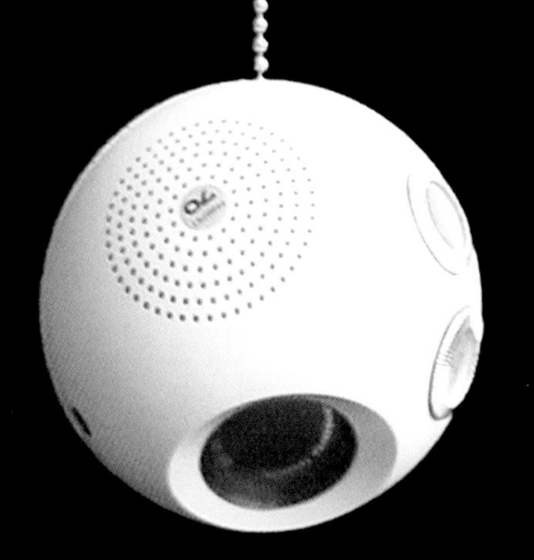

Panapet 70 transistor radios, Panasonic (Japan), each 5" diameter. Adorable and portable, the Panapet radio can be found in red, green, white, yellow, blue, and rare lavender. *Photo courtesy of designaddict.com.*

Joe Colombo KD 24 and KD 8 lamps for Kartell (Italy), both from the '60s, have movable shades that allow control over the degree of illumination. *Photos courtesy of designaddict.com.*

Chrome arms branch from a vibrant blue enameled base in this floor lamp from the 1970s. *Photo courtesy of Wright.*

Switching on these "rock lamps" manufactured by Singletron (Rome) in the 1970s transforms them from lumps of cast plastic with a granular surface into globes of light. *Photo courtesy of Wright.*

Accented by a green rug that suggests a patch of grass, this room in the home of Belgian collectors Patrick and Alix Everaert features the Joe Colombo Elda lounge chair for Comfort (Italy), 1963. *Photo courtesy of designaddict.com.*

Anna Castelli Ferrieri stacking units dominate Patrick and Alix Everaert's dining room, a cornucopia of '60s and '70s delights. Against the wall at far right, a tower of Joe Colombo KD 27 lamps provides an artful lighting option. *Photo courtesy of designaddict.com.*

This 1966 metal lounge chair with fabric upholstery is the largest of the chairs designed by Warren Platner for Knoll. *Photo courtesy of Wright.*

Shown here is a three-piece Wire System seating arrangement designed by Verner Panton for Fritz Hansen (Denmark), 1971. The seats can be used singly as chairs or combined to form a couch. *Photo courtesy of Marlon Gobel.*

In the home of Patrick and Alix Everaert, Verner Panton hanging lamps cluster over a rug by the same designer. On their encyclopedic Web site, designaddict.com, the Everaerts catalog the nearly six hundred items in their private collection. In addition, designaddict.com offers other virtual exhibits, designer interviews, an extensive bibliography, a design forum, and free ads for collectors. *Photo courtesy of designaddict.com.*

Glass designed for Orrefors (Sweden) by Olle Alberius (vases with internal stripes, early '70s) and Gunnar Cyren (goblets, 1967). *Photo courtesy of Wright.*

Easy-to-find and affordable Max 1 tableware by Lella and Massimo Vignelli for Heller (U.S.A.), 1964. *Photo courtesy of Fremont Antique Mall.*

This hand-woven wool carpet designed and signed by Alexander Calder was made in India ca. 1968. Calder is best known for his sculptures, particularly the famous mobiles and stabiles. *Photo courtesy of Wright.*

Three umbrella stands (left to right): 4650 by Gino Colombini for Kartell, 1965; Pluvium by Giancarlo Piretti for Anonima Castelli, 1972; and Noe by Bertoli & Pajetta for Fontana Arte, 1972. *Photo courtesy of Erica George Dines.*

Vico Magistretti's Eclisse lamp for Artemide (Italy), lacquered aluminum, 7" high, 1969. This fabulous piece won the Compasso d'Oro, an Italian industrial-design award. The white inner sphere can be rotated to expose or "eclipse" the bulb inside. A recently reissued version features a dial under the internal shade so that you can rotate it without burning your fingers; however, collectors prefer the original. *Photo courtesy of designaddict.com.*

NOW THAT YOU'RE READY TO START COLLECTING

You've read this far and are convinced that collecting '60s and '70s decor is for you. But before you rush out the door, checkbook in hand, take a moment to arm yourself with some inside information (and a few tools) that will help you find the best pieces and get the most for your money.

The Collector's Toolbox

When experienced collectors go to antiques shows and flea markets, they take along much more than a checkbook. These tools can help you evaluate a piece and then transport it home safely if you decide to make it yours.

- **Flashlight.** A flashlight is a valuable tool in any venue for close examination of almost any kind of item. Shop or mall lighting may not be brilliant enough to view the condition of a finish or to see the inside or underside of a piece.
- **Camera, notebook, and tape measure.** Affordably priced, easy-to-use point-and-click cameras make it simple to take pictures of a piece in which you're interested—to serve as a visual reference for further research or just to refresh your memory in case you decide to pursue a purchase after the show. Use your tape measure to record the measurements if

you need an idea of how the piece will fit into your living space. Etiquette requires getting the seller's permission before photographing or measuring a piece.

- **Tote bag and belt pack.** Remember that flea markets and garage sales aren't shopping malls—many sellers won't have bags with them. Taking your own tote bag is especially important at larger flea markets, where you may have to park some distance away. A zippered belt pack for your money, business cards, and receipts will save you the hassle of rifling through your wallet or purse to retrieve and file these things.
- **Wrapping and packing materials.** Also be sure to take some type of wrapping for your items. Clean newsprint, bubble wrap, and even paper towels can help protect your newfound treasures. Wrap items carefully, especially if you're packing several fragile pieces in the same bag. Keep a moving blanket or two (and perhaps some empty boxes) in the trunk of your car to cushion larger pieces.

What Determines the Value of a Piece?

Finding pieces you'd like to add to your collection is easy. Finding them at the right price takes a bit more work. Each of the following attributes has some impact on a piece's value—and therefore the price you'll pay.

Condition

The best possible condition for an item is the "unused dead stock" or "mint in the box" condition. At the opposite end of the spectrum are pieces so worn or damaged that they're no longer able to represent their original aesthetic; unless these are so rare that any example will have collectible value, they probably have no place in a serious collection.

More likely, you'll find pieces in between these extremes—ones in "good vintage" condition. By that we mean that a piece shows some signs of wear but is free from major problems that would rob it of its original aesthetic, such as discoloration, cracks, chips, or missing pieces. Unfortunately, you'll probably come across your share of pieces that have seen better days—ones whose owners viewed them more as throwaways than as potentially valuable collectibles. A case in point: the Panasonic Toot-a-Loop transistor radios that were so popular and, accordingly, heavily used.

Damage

As a collector, your goal should be to look for pieces that appear to have been well cared for their whole life. Although they'll likely show some signs of wear, they'll be free of the kind of obvious or major damage that would detract from the piece as a whole. And don't forget to factor in how you plan to use a piece. For example, if you're looking for Heller plastic dinnerware to display as showpieces in your collection, nothing short of perfect condition may do. But if your plan is to use the pieces at meals every day, a few scratches shouldn't be a problem.

As you shop, be on the lookout the following common types of damage.

- **Normal usage wear.** Expect vintage objects to show signs of normal wear. As long as the wear is negligible, the effect on value will be minimal.
- **Unusual usage wear.** Deep scratches, melt marks, or heavy sun discoloration can have a significant effect on value. A piece with such unusual usage wear may be worth only 30 to 75 percent of what a good vintage example might command.
- **Dust and dirt.** Fortunately, because most '60s and '70s collectibles were made of synthetic materials, dust and dirt generally respond to careful cleaning.
- **Discoloration.** This is simply a fact of life for the collector of '60s and '70s design. Slight, even discoloration on white plastics is acceptable to most collectors and may reduce a piece's value by only 10 to 20 percent.
- **Sun damage.** Colored plastics will fade when exposed to sunlight, and usually not evenly. Interestingly, this kind of discoloration has a greater effect on value than comparable discoloration of white plastics—anywhere from a 20 to 40 percent reduction—perhaps because it's more disruptive to the original aesthetic of the piece.
- **Chips and cracks.** If chips or cracks are visible and/or they affect the structural integrity of a piece, the item's value may be reduced by as much as 50 to 70 percent. If the damage is

restricted to an area that's not readily visible, the impact on value will be less.

- **Scratches, dents, gouges, tears, and punctures.** Like chips and cracks, these are major kinds of damage. Expect a reduction in value of anywhere from 40 to 60 percent.

Missing or Replaced Parts

An item that has all of its original components is usually worth more than a similar one that's incomplete or has had parts replaced. But even in the latter case, it's somewhat of a judgment call. For example, if a vintage television in otherwise good condition is simply missing a knob or the tip of its antenna, it's often possible to replace the items with identical ones from a "junker" example of the same model.

Philco (U.S.A.) B370ETG television, ca. 1972. *Photo courtesy of Fremont Antique Mall.*

However, if a missing part is integral to the piece—such as an unusual shade on a vintage lamp—it may be difficult to find an exact replacement. And anything less may render the lamp undesirable to the collector. An exception might be a piece of furniture whose upholstery is so worn or damaged that it begs for replacement. In that case, reupholstering with a new fabric that's in the same style as the original may actually add to the piece's value.

Functionality

What if an item you'd like to buy no longer works? Is it still worth owning, and if so, at what price?

In the field of '60s and '70s collectibles, this question comes up most often with electronics. And interestingly, collectors are somewhat divided about the importance of a piece's being in working condition. Certainly, a radio you can listen to as well as just look at is always preferable. But if you plan to use the piece only decoratively, outward appearance may be more important to you than functionality. And even if they're in working order, European electronics may not function in the United States due to differences in broadcast frequencies and systems.

Repairs and Restoration

Most collectors will buy pieces that have been repaired to some degree. And a piece that's been restored to its original condition without the addition of any new materials is still a good investment and should be worth only slightly less than an unrestored example. That said, there are precious few instances where repair and restoration are possible with most '60s and '70s collectibles. Plastics are difficult to restore with conventional methods. The same is true for glass, metal, and ceramic.

A possible exception is fiberglass. Auto-body shops and others experienced with fiberglass may be able to repair the shell on a piece of furniture or apply a new gel coat to the shell's surface. To many collectors, these repairs will be acceptable because they'll enhance the object's appearance for everyday use. But if you're looking beyond mere appearance and utility to a piece's future value, you'd be better served to wait for an example that's in pristine original condition, however much more you may have to pay for it.

Because the pieces that collectors of '60s and '70s design pursue aren't that old, it's usually not too difficult to find examples in good condition. Don't feel pressured to purchase an inferior example out of fear that a better one won't come along. It will.

Original Packaging

Unlike collectible toys and dolls, most examples of '60s and '70s design aren't significantly more valuable if their boxes or original packaging are intact. An exception to this rule is when the packaging itself has intrinsic value because of its design or graphics (and is still in good condition).

When you do occasionally find lighting, small plastic furnishings, tableware, or electronics still in the original packaging, it may be an indication that the item was seldom if ever used or was especially well cared for. In that case, the item may indeed be more valuable, but not simply because of the box.

Why Collectors Love Labels

Even though most collectors don't get particularly excited about finding a piece in its original box, their pulse quickens when that piece sports an original tag, label, or sticker. That little slip of paper is worth nothing by itself, but the information on it can add considerably to a piece's value.

Some stickers, such as those used by Raymor, a distributor of modern design, will indicate the actual manufacturer of the item. In other cases, a sticker or label will pinpoint when an item was produced, which can be important for pieces that have been manufactured over a long period. Usually, the earliest examples command the highest prices.

Intrinsic Characteristics

Exactly what is it that makes one piece from this period a sought-after example of documented design and another a mere curiosity? There are probably as many answers as there are collectors, but here are some of the things that strike a common chord.

- **Period representation.** It's hard to overestimate the importance that exemplifying the period has on a piece's value. Designs that are more generic are always less prized.
- **Unusual design.** The '60s and '70s were all about being free to experiment with new forms, so the best examples of unusual design typically command the highest prices.
- **Rare colors.** Collectors seek out the brightest and rarest colors, especially orange, lime green, and yellow. For the JVC Videosphere television, orange and black are the colors most seldom seen and therefore the most valuable.
- **Attribution.** Pieces from designers such as Verner Panton, Joe Colombo, Anna Castelli Ferrieri, Achille Castiglioni, and Raymond Loewy (among numerous others) are perennial favorites.
- **Theme.** Perhaps because they're so representative of the decades that spawned them, pieces with a space-age or pop-art theme are always in high demand.

Age

With most examples of '60s and '70s design, age isn't a critical factor. After all, we're dealing with pieces designed over a fifteen-year period and manufactured only thirty years ago. Age is an issue only in determining that they are indeed from the period.

As a collector, you'll soon develop an eye for true vintage examples. One of the first things you'll want to do is find out whether the piece is still in production. The Internet has made this much easier: most manufacturers have Web sites that illustrate their current production.

From there, look at the following attributes, singly and in combination, to help determine a piece's age.

- The manufacturer's stamp, label, or mark.
- The trademark.
- Manufacturers' original catalogs (or reprints of them).
- The dealer's claims or representations.
- Stylistic references.
- Published references in vintage design magazines and decorating books.

The Collector as Detective

Let's say you've just found a few Kartell Round-Up stacking units, designed by Anna Castelli Ferrieri, at a flea market. Since you happen to know these units are still being made, how can you tell if these examples are vintage or current production?

First, trust your eyes. Very few thirty-year-old plastic furnishings appear on the market without some signs of wear. Next, look at the color of plastic. Pop colors such as green, yellow, orange, lavender, and chrome were produced only prior to 1975. Earth tones like mushroom, brown, and avocado were introduced in the late '70s, and baby blue, cosmetic pink, and magenta were introduced in the 1980s. Red and black were made until just a few years ago, and white has remained in production since day one.

Finally, look at the molded marking. As the injection molds age and have to be replaced, subtle changes appear here. For example, until 1979, Kartell licensed a domestic manufacturer, Beylerian, to produce its more popular products for the American market. Therefore, if a piece bears the Beylerian mark, you know it predates 1979.

Rarity

In any field of collecting, the rarest examples are the collector's treasures. And even though it's barely thirty years old, '60s and '70s design already can lay claim to a few of them—but for decidedly different reasons.

- **Some were commercial failures.** Some furniture designs were so radical for their time that they didn't sell well, so relatively few were made. Others were from small manufacturers which simply didn't have the capacity to produce on a large scale.
- **Some were deemed too commonplace.** Well-designed household items like dustpans, rug beaters, strainers, and electric fans simply weren't saved. Because they were utilitarian, they were sometimes considered commonplace.
- **Some became technological dinosaurs.** As personal electronics became more sophisticated, the "silly" space-age designs of the '70s were cast aside.
- **Some went out of style.** The growing importance of fashion took a toll on objects that were used only as long as they were thought to be in style. In 1971, there was little reason to think that the set of Heller dishes you bought to use on the patio would someday be collectible.

Attribution

The hands that touched an item can have a big impact on its value, and '60s and '70s objects by known designers typically sell for the highest prices and retain the highest values. How much higher? That's difficult to say. A very rare object by a more obscure designer might fetch more than a common object by a better-known designer.

In any case, before paying a premium price for a piece based primarily on its association with a designer's name, insist on definitive documentation. Plastic items from Artemide and Kartell are often impressed with the name of the manufacturer and designer as well as the year and country of origin. On other pieces, a paper or foil label or a name plaque may appear. In the absence of any identification, you may be able to verify designer attribution with vintage manufacturers' catalogs and reference books.

The Rarest of the Rare

If you should be lucky enough to inherit an old Archizoom Safari sofa when your aunt Edna remodels her basement rec room, think twice before setting it out on the curb for the trashman. At auction, it could command more than $30,000.

Another rarity from the '60s is the Elephant chair designed by Bernard Rancillac. Until 1966, it was offered only in an initial edition of twenty (the designer authorized a second edition of one hundred in 1985). Even the reissues have sold at auction for as much as $6,000.

Provenance

Is a piece's value enhanced simply because of its provenance, or history of ownership? That has certainly been true in other areas of collecting. But the field of '60s and '70s design is still so new, we'll have to wait a bit longer to find out. Many famous people are known to collect '60s and '70s furnishings—Lenny Kravitz's Miami house, for example, has been featured in design magazines—and someday when those collections are seen at auction, provenance may indeed have an impact on their value.

Dealing with Knockoffs, Fakes, Reproductions, and Reissues

A knockoff is an unauthorized copy of a piece in which the design is slightly altered (usually cheapened) in order to avoid having to pay royalties to the designer or his estate. Most knockoffs are of little interest to collectors; they don't exhibit the same attention to detail in the manufacturing and modeling that true vintage pieces do.

Common examples of period knockoffs are the many beanbag chairs inspired by the Sacco chair (designed by Piero Gatti, Cesare Paolini, and Franco Teodoro for Zanotta in 1969) and Taiwanese inflatable chairs inspired by the "Blow" chair (designed by Gionatan De Pas, Donato D'Urbino, and Paola Lomazzi for Zanotta in 1967). As a collector, you'll soon develop an eye for original designs and quality manufacturing. In the meantime, whenever you're unsure of the authenticity of a piece you're considering, always ask the seller: "How can I verify that this is what you say it is?"

COLLECTOR'S COMPASS

Names to Know

Anna Castelli Ferrieri (Italian, born 1920). Anna Castelli Ferrieri was among the most influential designers of the period. Her modular storage units, furniture, shelving, kitchenware, and tableware epitomize the design concepts of the period. From the mid-1960s, her position as design consultant, and later art director, at Kartell meant she supervised much of the company's design selection.

Joe Colombo (Italian, 1930–71). The quintessential designer of the period, Colombo is known for innovations that extended to furniture, appliances, glass, lighting, and interiors. His work for clients such as Kartell, Comfort, and Italora are marked by economy of design, versatility of use, and exploitation of new technologies. Many consider his premature death in 1971 the beginning of the end for design of the period.

Vico Magistretti (Italian, born 1920). This Milanese architect was one of the first Italian designers to consider plastic a suitable material for mass-produced objects and furnishings using completely mechanized production systems. He was awarded the prestigious Compasso d'Oro award for his Eclisse lamp (1967 for Artemide), Maralunga chair (1973 for Cassina), Atollo lamp (1977 for O'Luce), and Gaudi armchair (1979 for Artemide).

Verner Panton (Danish, 1926–99). Panton, who worked as an associate of Arne Jacobsen's before starting his own firm in 1955, is known for truly innovative furniture designs that utilized new technologies and expanded the parameters of design. His single-form chair of 1960 is an icon of modern design. He's also recognized for lighting (for Louis Poulsen), rugs and textiles, and coordinated interiors. His work often reflects a strong op-art influence.

For a quick visual reference to the work of these and hundreds of other designers active in this period, visit www.tribu-design.com.

Vico Magistretti's Selene stackable chair for Artemide (Italy), 1969.
Photo courtesy of designaddict.com.

> *To Learn More*
> *L' Utopie du Tout Plastique 1960–1973*, Fondation pour l'Architecture, Brussels, 1994

Fakes are a bit more difficult to spot because their intent is to deceive. Two well-known examples are the fake Molar and Castle chairs (originals by Wendell Castle) manufactured in Florida in the early 1990s. Since the perpetrator used the same production techniques and materials as the originals, the fakes are virtually impossible to distinguish from the chairs produced for Stendig in 1969. (These imitations eventually inspired Castle to put his designs back into legitimate production in 1998.)

Reproductions and reissues are currently available from several original manufacturers, and there may be instances when you'll want to add such pieces to your collection. For example, if you really desire white plastic pieces but without the discoloration common on vintage examples, you might choose to go with current production. The technologies used in the formulation of plastics have improved exponentially over the past forty years, and today's plastic furniture is much more chemically stable and light-safe.

As appreciation for the designs of the period continues to grow, more and more manufacturers have reissued classic designs. Artemide has introduced a line called Artemide Classics, bringing back several long-out-of-production designs. And design galleries have even reissued limited editions of pieces that originally were produced only on a very small scale.

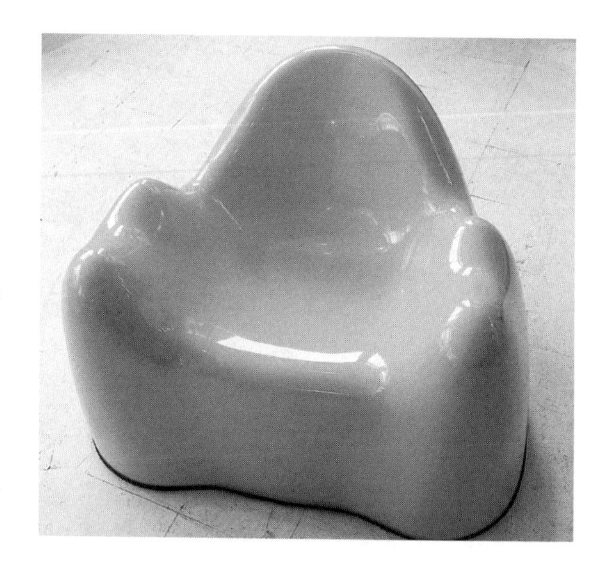

Wendell Castle's Molar chair, fiberglass, 1971. In the '60s and '70s, new manufacturing techniques made almost any shape possible, and Castle took full advantage to create this playful pop-art tooth. *Photo courtesy of Area 51.*

Building Your Collection

As a novice collector of '60s and '70s design, you may be vexed by questions about everything from deciding what to buy to what to do with pieces once you own them. Fortunately, many other collectors have asked themselves the same questions and are more than happy to share their advice.

How should I display my collection?

No surprise—the plastic and pop designs of the '60s and '70s don't really mix well with French provincial, early American, and other decors. That's why many collectors have chosen to display their collections as an entire landscape of furnishings and decorative objects—together in a single room or throughout their homes. It's hard to deny the impact of walking into a home filled with furnishings in lime, tangerine, and lemon, where floating chairs hang from the ceiling and floor-hugging lamps have the appearance of glowing rocks!

How big might my collection get?

In every field of collecting, there are devotees with the time and budget to amass huge collections. Although these collections are admirable for their size and thoroughness, they aren't what most collectors aspire to.

In the field of '60s and '70s design, one outstanding collection formed the basis for the *L'Utopie du Tout Plastique* book and later became the Plasticarium Museum in Brussels. Another well-known collection, also in Belgium, is the personal holdings of Patrick and Alix Everaert (known as the P&A Collection). It has been fully documented and can be viewed online, item by item, at www.designaddict.com. The Everaerts' Web site contains more than one thousand pages of pictures and information about design and decor of the period.

Should I try to collect broadly or cherry-pick for only the best pieces?

As your collection develops, it's only natural that there will be pieces that stand out from the others—perhaps because of their value, rarity, condition, or great stories about their acquisition.

It can be difficult (if not impossible) to assemble a collection that's uniformly outstanding, and in fact that may be a good thing. If you plan on using your furnishings in your home, as many collectors do, you may not want to go to the expense of buying a mint-condition example of every piece; even with only your own use, they're not likely to stay that way. Instead, try to evaluate each potential acquisition in the context of the rest of your collection and how you intend to use it.

Are there currently any bargains in the field of '60s and '70s design?

Regrettably, there seem to be fewer all the time. But many people are still in the dark about the value of '60s and '70s designs, so the occasional bargain can still be had. Your best ally is a broad general knowledge of the field so you'll be prepared to recognize and take advantage of these bargains when you find them.

On the other hand, it could be argued that vintage designer furnishings are a bargain in themselves. If you buy well, you can often recoup your investment. When you go to a typical furniture store and buy attractive but anonymous new pieces, they will have almost no resale value. Six months later, you'd be lucky to get 30 percent of what you paid. However, there's a much better chance that documented-design classic furniture will hold its value. If you decide ten years from now to change to Victorian or French Empire decor, you won't lose your shirt or, worse, simply end up junking your old pieces.

How can I improve on the pieces I've already collected?

Over time, you'll probably have the opportunity to sell items you're ready to part with and thereby afford better pieces to take their place. Those opportunities are good times to rethink what you want from your collection. Are you trying to find a number of pieces to furnish a new apartment or house? Or are you more interested in seeking only the most outstanding examples of a few showpiece designs?

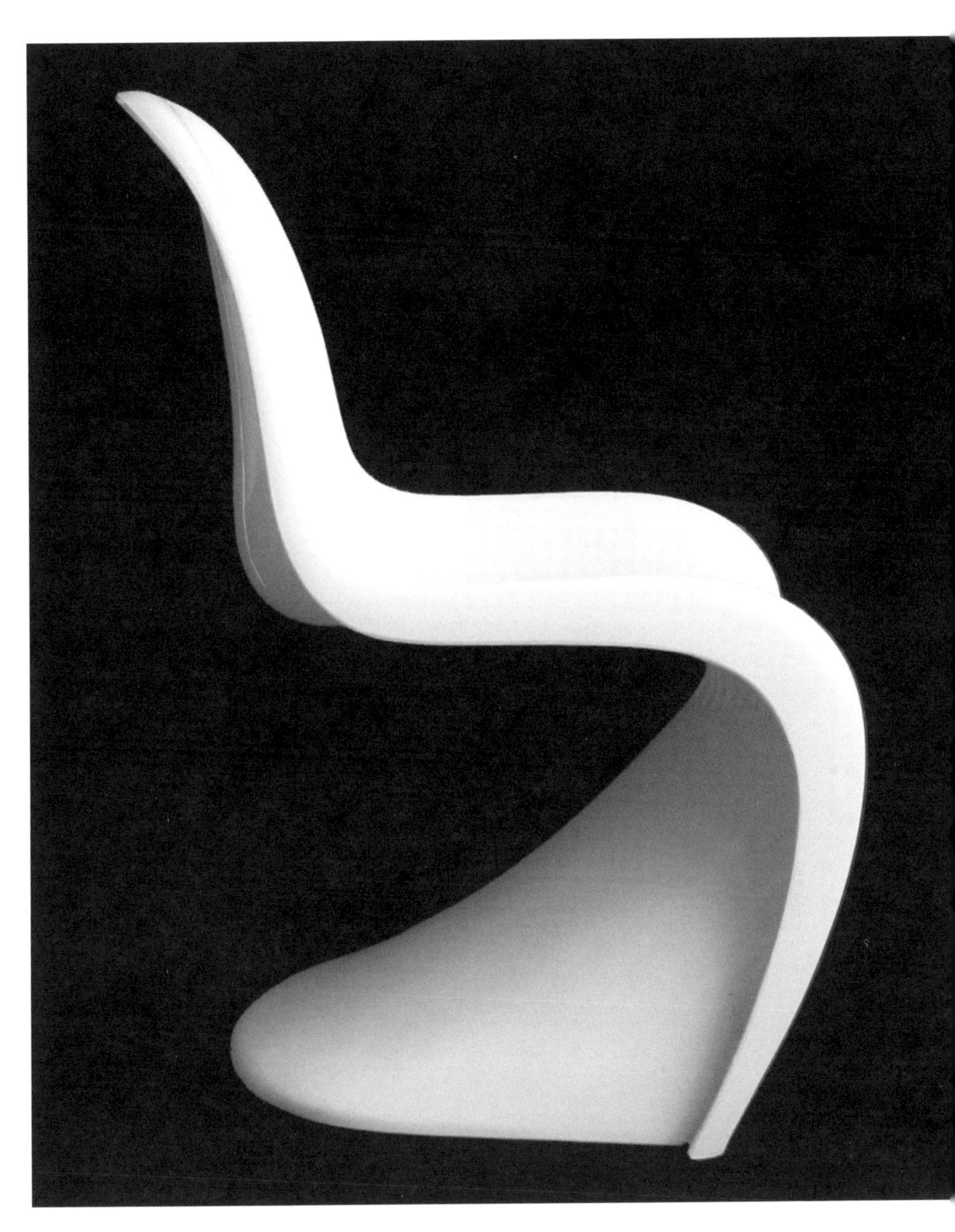

A vintage example of Verner Panton's iconic Cantilever chair for Herman Miller (U.S.A.). This original version was made of ABS plastic; later reissues by Vitra (Switzerland) differ in materials and construction. *Photo courtesy of designaddict.com.*

What records should I keep?

It's important to maintain accurate and up-to-date records to document and protect the value of your collection.

- **Receipts.** Whenever possible, retain the original dated receipt for each item you acquire.
- **Dealer contacts.** You may need to recontact the dealer because of a problem with a piece, or you may want to sell back or trade up with the same dealer or have him watch out for a particular item.
- **A collection inventory.** Whether you go low-tech with a simple handwritten notebook or opt to use a dedicated software program for collectibles (Primasoft Collectibles Organizer is a good one), you'll want to note the date each item was purchased; the name, address, and phone number of the seller; a description of the item, including the designer's name, the style, shape, pattern, color, and dimensions; the item's condition; and the purchase price. If the seller made any guarantees concerning the item, note those too.
- **Photos and videotapes.** Photos and videos let you record details about your collection that you may never think to make note of, and they could be key to filing an insurance claim in the event of a loss. With digital technology, it's now easy to store your photos on your computer's hard drive.

Keeping good records is one thing; protecting them is another. Be sure to keep a backup copy of your inventory program, and to store it along with receipts and photographic records in a safe place off premises, such as a safe-deposit box at your bank.

Do I need an appraisal?

An appraisal (or valuation as it's also called) is a formal evaluation of an object or collection made by a professional who's an expert in the field. An appraisal should include the value of the piece, as well as a full description covering size, material, vintage, manufacturer, and condition. An appraisal should be presented on the letterhead of the firm and be signed by the person who conducted it.

A formal appraisal may be required for insurance purposes if your collection has increased significantly in value. You'll need an appraisal if you're donating an object to a charity or public collection and will claim a tax deduction. And if you should inherit a collection whose value you're unsure of, an appraisal is definitely in order to establish its worth and secure the necessary insurance coverage.

Remember, an appraisal is only as accurate as the person who provides it. An expert in Art Deco may know little about '60s and '70s design. Start your search for a reputable, knowledgeable appraiser with fellow collectors, dealers, auction houses, and these recognized appraisal groups:

- **The International Society of Appraisers**
  www.isa-appraisers.org; 888-472-5587
- **The American Society of Appraisers**
  www.appraisers.org; 800-ASA-VALU; 703-478-2228
- **The Appraisers Association of America**
  www.appraisersassoc.org; 212-889-5404

Should I carry separate insurance on my collection?

That depends. You will need to weigh the cost of the insurance against the value of your collection and the financial impact you'd suffer if you lost it. Some regular homeowner's policies cover collections. Others require a special rider or even a separate policy. In making your decision, take into account the total value of your collection, the types of items you collect, and the specific terms of your present policy.

TR-005 Orbitel TV, Panasonic, 1970. Silver and sleek, this flying-saucer-shaped television embodies all the excitement of the space age. *Photo courtesy of Erica George Dines.*

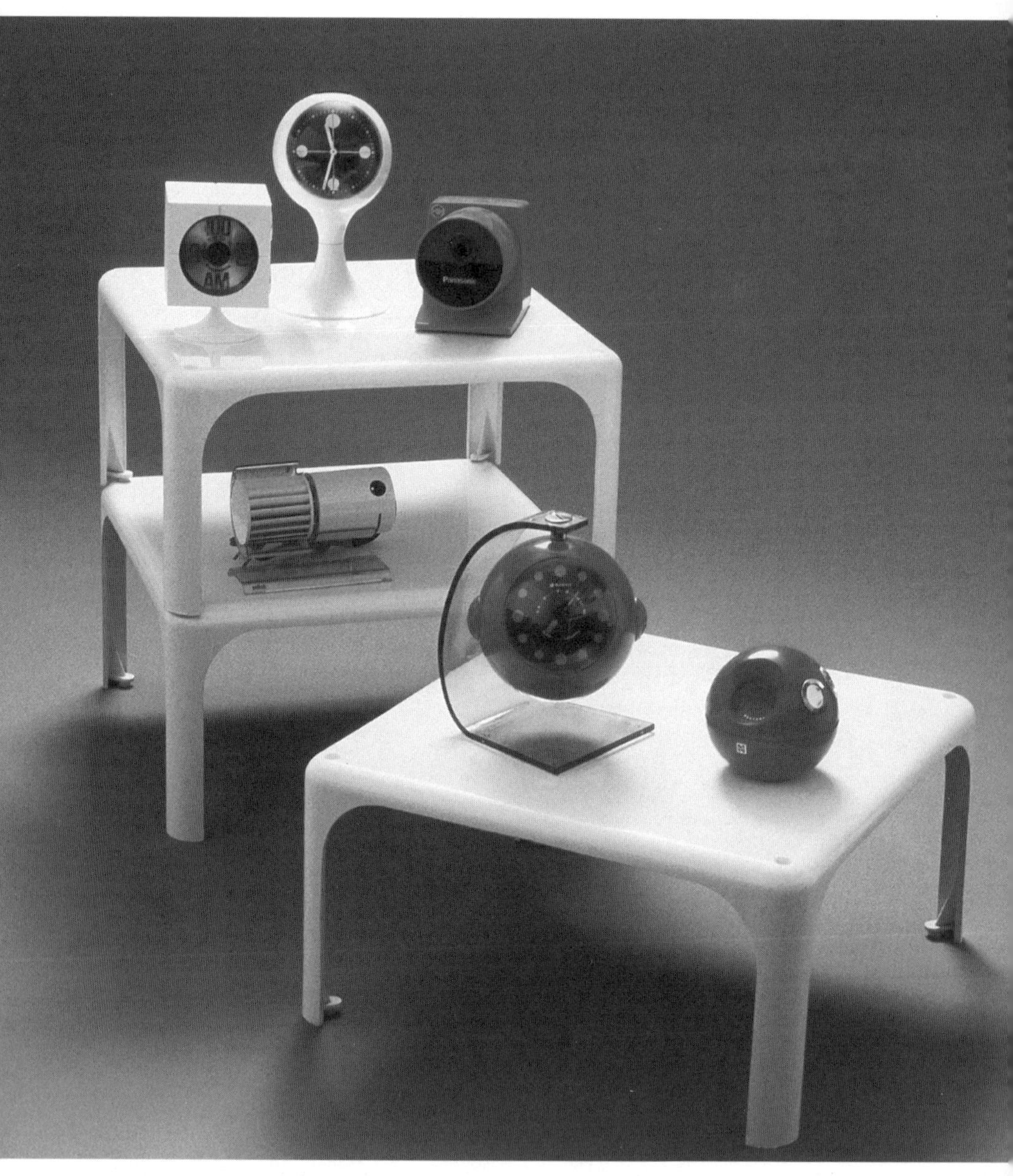

Vico Magistretti's Demetrio 45 tables for Artemide (Italy), 1966, offer stackable display space for '60s and '70s electronics. On the rear tables, from left to right and top to bottom, are a Cube radio (Panasonic, 1970), table clock (Endura, ca. 1970), Panapoint pencil sharpener (Panasonic, 1972), and HL70 desk fan (Braun, 1971). A table clock (Sanyo, 1970), and Panapet 70 radio rest on the table in front. *Photo courtesy of Erica George Dines.*

LIVING WITH YOUR COLLECTION

With its bright colors, unusual materials, and futuristic shapes, nothing seems to brighten a room—or draw quite as much attention from guests—as '60s and '70s decor. That's why most collectors wouldn't think of putting their pieces in display cases to be admired from a distance—they'd rather live with them. From the bookcases that hold their design reference books to the accessories on their desks, right down to the plates they eat from, they integrate their collections into nearly every aspect of their lives.

"Why Do I Collect '60s and '70s Decor?"
Here's how one collector answers the question.

"One of the main reasons I collect this style is that it's fun to look at and to live with. It's uplifting and at the same time quite useful. And it reflects a casual lifestyle that works very well in today's homes. At one point, the majority of my loft apartment was decorated with '60s and '70s pieces. The plastic freestanding shelving units were certainly useful in this space because storage areas were scarce. The modular seating system that could convert into a bed was perfect, since the large space was without a separate bedroom. And the space-age electronics made good shelf 'sculpture' that always brought comments from visitors."

Displaying, Protecting, and Storing Your Collection

What's the best way to display my pieces?

That depends on the pieces themselves. Because '60s and '70s decor includes everything from shelving and sofas to artwork and textiles—and more—much depends on how you'll use and live with your items. You'll probably want to display your furniture, lighting, and decorating accessories in room settings. Small pieces such as collectible electronics work equally well as tabletop accents or grouped en masse on a shelf or in a display case for big impact.

Showing Your Pieces in Their Best Light

Because so many '60s and '70s pieces were made of various forms of plastic, which can discolor with prolonged exposure to the ultraviolet rays of the sun, lighting your collection is a bit of a balancing act. You want to show it at its best yet protect it from damage. Fluorescent lighting can cause plastics to break down—and the heat from halogen lamps can cause them to melt!

If you've ever found plastic Kartell furniture units in almond or reddish-orange, you've already seen the damage that improper lighting can do. When new, the units were almost certainly bright white and rich tomato red!

What can I do to protect my collection from sunlight and extremes of temperature and humidity?

Primarily, just use good common sense. As you've just read, sunlight is an enemy of plastic. So you'll naturally want to use appropriate window coverings to protect plastic furnishings. The same goes for fabrics on upholstered furniture and for wall hangings, curtains, bedspreads, and tablecloths.

Temperature extremes and moisture are other culprits to guard against. Extreme heat can soften and even melt some plastics, and frigid cold can make plastics brittle and more susceptible to cracking and breaking. Chrome accents on furniture and accessories won't remain in like-new condition in a moist or humid environment.

Are there areas or rooms of my house where I shouldn't store or display my collection?

Most definitely, and you probably already know what they are: garages, attics, and basements, where temperature extremes, moisture, and humidity will wreak havoc on just about anything you put there. But close on their heels are bathrooms, where humidity can destroy the interior workings of electronics you might think of displaying there, and kitchens (and adjacent areas), where airborne grease can, at the very least, make cleaning your pieces a nightmare.

Although originally intended for a corporate environment, a 1972 ensemble of sofa, table, and chairs by American manufacturer Steelcraft has been put to comfortable use in dealer Marlon Gobel's apartment. A Karuselli armchair from Finnish company Haimi-Oy coordinates perfectly, and an orange-upholstered wire seating arrangement designed by Verner Panton completes the room. *Photo courtesy of Marlon Gobel.*

New Life for Old Fiberglass

One type of plastic that lends itself to professional repair is fiberglass. Fiberglass is composed of a base material of spun-glass fibers, which is then covered by a synthetic gel coat. This gel coat eventually can become worn or damaged.

If you have a piece of fiberglass furniture in need of repair, an automotive shop or boatyard may be able to restore or replace the damaged gel coat. Be aware, though, that such a repair will reduce the piece's value in much the same way as refinishing a piece of vintage wood furniture.

What if I collect too many pieces to display or store at home?

If the collecting bug truly bites you, there'll probably be no "what if" about it. Eventually, your collection will outgrow house and home.

When that happens, it's time to go shopping for good off-site storage for the pieces you can't display but can't bear to part with. Here are some tips from seasoned collectors on how to proceed.

- Look for an indoor storage facility with a temperature- and humidity-controlled environment. A security guard should be on duty around the clock to ensure the safety of your items.
- Carefully pack and wrap your items for storage. Investing in sturdy new cardboard boxes and lots of bubble wrap and plastic peanuts will simplify the job of packing smaller pieces. Blankets (from thrift stores) and packing quilts are best for protecting large furniture pieces.
- Take care not to overpack your boxes; the contents may break through the bottom.
- Stack boxes only to a reasonable height. Avoid stacking boxes on top of delicate or upholstered furniture pieces.

How concerned should I be about the security of my collection?

Luckily, most thieves don't know the value of modern collectibles. There seems to be little demand for plastic furniture—unlike silver and jewelry—on the black market! Still, you'll want to take all necessary precautions to protect your home from theft and to document and insure your collection. And it's a good idea not to brag in public about just how valuable some of your pieces are.

Cleaning and Caring for Your Collection

Are there any special dos and don'ts for cleaning my pieces?

The most important rule is a simple one: Always try to get by with the gentlest cleaning agents possible. Often, the best cleaner is mild soap in warm water applied with a soft rag. Only if that does not work should you try one of the following cleaners formulated for specific materials. Always test first on an inconspicuous spot.

- Rigid opaque plastics and fiberglass respond well to commercial plastic polishes (Novous is a popular brand).
- Automotive products like Armor-All and No. 7 White Polishing Compound will restore the finish on older plastics. Note: Black plastics and polypropylene (a soft plastic with a waxy-looking finish) shouldn't be polished with an abrasive cleaner.
- To remove the adhesive residue from price stickers and tape, use a product called Goo-Gone.
- Soft Scrub with Bleach works well on enameled pieces such as lamps.
- Use K2R Spot Lifter on draperies, carpets, tablecloths, and other fabrics.
- Hagerty Silver Foaming Polish will restore the finish on silver and silver-plated objects.

Repair and Restoration

I have a few pieces that need small repairs. Should I try to make them myself?

Probably not. The goal of a collector should be to maintain a piece in a condition as close to the original as possible. Even professional repairs may be a step in the wrong direction, not to mention botched attempts by an amateur.

The sole exceptions may be the replacement of a missing part (such as a knob on a vintage television) or the simple rewiring of a nonworking lamp (but only if you've already had some experience with electrical repairs).

Olivier Mourgue's Djinn chair for Airborne, 1965. In Stanley Kubrick's *2001: A Space Odyssey,* Mourgue's red Djinn chairs lent futuristic elegance to the Space Hilton. The chair shown here was featured in the "2001: A Space Odyssey Collectibles Exhibit" at the San Mateo, California, public library in 1999. More Mourgue pieces and other *2001* collectibles can be seen online at www.2001exhibit.org. *Photo by Mark Watson, courtesy of Dennis Gonzales.*

What if a piece I own or want to buy needs major repairs?

If it's a piece you want to buy, think twice. Unless it's so rare that you'd be happy to have any example of it, no matter how poor the condition, seasoned collectors advise against buying pieces that need major repair.

On the other hand, if you already own the piece and simply want to continue using it, you may not be very concerned with its future value. In that case, go ahead and have an auto-body shop give that Eero Aarnio Gyro chair a new bright white gel coat or reupholster your Olivier Mourgue Djinn sofa in a vintage fabric or a new one with a vintage look. In the latter case, the reupholstering, if done well, may not diminish the collectible value of the piece at all.

I have a piece I'd like to repair, even though I know it might not be worth the cost. What should I do?

Again, that depends. How concerned are you with preserving the piece's value and marketability? For example, there's a "don't ever" rule about caring for '60s and '70s plastic furniture: Don't ever paint it! You may make the piece look much nicer, but you'll also make it impossible to sell on the collectors' market.

That said, if the piece is already so discolored that it has lost most of its value, you may decide that painting it and simply using it decoratively is just fine. (If you do, here's a tip: Use ordinary spray enamel, and apply several very thin coats to avoid drips and puddles.)

Other Concerns

Are there any health or safety concerns I should be aware of with '60s and '70s collectibles?

You should know that some plastics from this period were manufactured using toxic chemicals. Some people feel that it's possible for these chemicals to leach out of the plastic and cause harm. But it's doubtful that the chemicals pose any real threat, even to the most avid collector.

If you collect period electronics that you plan to use in your home, it would be a good idea to have any items originally manufactured and sold abroad checked by a licensed electrician.

The Fremont Antique Mall in Seattle, and others like it throughout the country, hold bargains for collectors of '60s and '70s design—and opportunities for selling pieces from a collection.

IF AND WHEN YOU DECIDE TO SELL

From Collector to Seller

As great as your passion for '60s and '70s decor may be, at some point you may want or need to sell some or all of your collection. When you do, you'll find that there are a variety of ways to go about it—some quicker than others, some more work than others, and some more likely than others to turn you a profit.

People's personal circumstances change. Perhaps your collecting budget is greater now than it was when you first started; today, scarcer and more desirable pieces are your game, and the more common ones you bought a few years ago no longer hold as much appeal. Perhaps you're contemplating financing a major purchase or expense—a new home, a college education, and so on—and the money you've invested in your collection needs to be freed up (if only for a time). Maybe you're downsizing your household, and you simply won't have the space you once enjoyed for your huge collection. Maybe your collection has just become too big to enjoy. Or perhaps you've moved into a different living space with a different "style" that doesn't complement your collection aesthetically.

Whatever your reason for selling, here's where good record keeping pays off. If you have every item in your collection described in a database or on a set of inventory forms, it will be easy to review what you have to sell. Being able to reference what you paid will help you set your prices. If you took care to capture the details of an item's condition, defects, and completeness, you've already gone a long way toward writing a listing—whether for an ad, a price tag, or an online auction.

You Want to Trade Up or Your Interest Has Changed

One of the most common reasons to sell is to trade up. Perhaps you've found an example in much better condition than the item you already own. Maybe you've zeroed in on your collecting specialty, and some of your pieces are outside the scope of that theme. You may have acquired duplicates in the course of buying large lots in order to get the few items you really needed. Maybe you've learned more about the pieces you've purchased so that you're less interested in some of them now. Or your tastes simply may have evolved.

What do you do with pieces you've outgrown? The next time you go to a collectibles show, try taking a couple of your "extra" pieces along to see if you can find a dealer who will buy or trade. It's largely a hit-or-miss proposition, but the worst-case scenario is that you may have to take the pieces back home at the end of the day. If you have a rare item, it's probably better to sell it than trade it.

You Need the Money

Selling your collection because you need the money is never an ideal situation, but let's face it: kids need braces and the college tuition has to be paid. More urgent situations like an illness, a job loss, or a move may also force you to sell. Again, if you've kept good records, you should be able to liquidate fairly quickly and find several different sales avenues to explore.

Sell Your Collection to a Dealer

Selling your collection to a dealer will probably net you the lowest return on the money you've invested, since dealers typically pay only a fraction of current market value—usually 50 percent or less. But if you've held your pieces for a long time, even the wholesale prices a dealer will pay could net you a gain over what you originally paid. Or you may be lucky enough to own items that have become much more desirable since you bought them.

If you live near a major metropolitan area, you may be better served by dealers there as opposed to in your local market. Demand and prices for '60s and '70s pieces are higher in metropolitan markets, and dealers will generally be able to pay you a better price as a result.

Depending on your circumstances, the speed, ease, and convenience of selling your collection as a whole may outweigh the money issue. You'll avoid many of the headaches of selling—keeping track of individual sales, and packing and shipping, not to mention bad checks, disgruntled purchasers, and being stuck with items that just won't move.

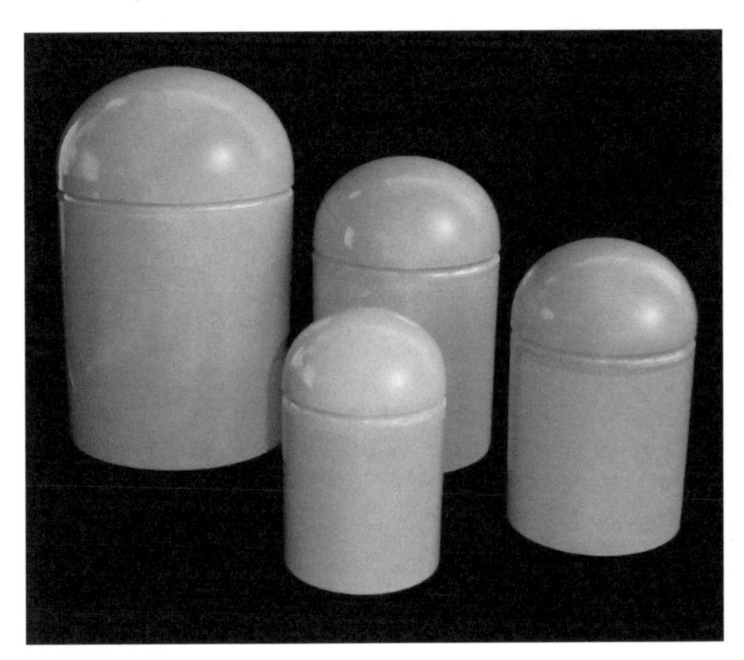

Anna Castelli Ferrieri 7301, 7302, 7303, and 7304 containers for Kartell (Italy); 6¼" to 11" high; 1969. *Photo courtesy of designaddict.com.*

Consign Your Collection to a Dealer

You may get more money for your collection by consigning to a dealer, but it will take you longer to sell it. If you go this route, you definitely need to have an item-by-item inventory and establish a specific price for each piece. You should also discuss your price expectations with the consignee: although the dealer is going to receive a percentage of the selling price as his commission, he'll

Emma Gismondi-Schweinberger's Giano Vano bedside table for Artemide (Italy), 1966. A variation, the Giano Vano Ruote, rests on casters for easy mobility. *Photo courtesy of designaddict.com.*

be reluctant to handle an item if you have unrealistic price expectations that may keep it in his inventory for too long. Clarify the details of your arrangement, which should be written down and signed by both of you.

One of the best reasons to enter into an arrangement like this is that full-time dealers cover more ground than you can—operating simultaneously at shows, in malls, and even on the Internet. They also have many more contacts and a supply of want lists from other collectors who are ready to buy. The commission you pay for access to the dealer's selling network is well worth it.

Sell Your Collection Yourself

Selling your collection yourself is the most time-consuming option, both in terms of the hours you'll have to put into it as well as how long it will take. Not only will you need to be on top of the market, you'll have to present your items for sale, establish a network of contacts as you look for potential customers, and—if you're selling by mail or online—follow through on every transaction. You'll be on the other side of customer-service issues and hassles such as bad checks, complaints, tracking shipments—the whole deal.

The Internet is the most popular venue for a self-seller, but it also has its drawbacks. If you use one of the big online auction sites such as eBay, Amazon, or Yahoo, and you make an innocent mistake or fail to hold up your end of a transaction, it might lead to a posting of negative feedback that will make other buyers wary of you. If you run an ad in a collectors' magazine, you'll have to put up money with no guarantee that you'll ever make it back. Also, the lead time for placing ads in magazines and trade papers can use up precious weeks before anyone even sees your ad.

On the plus side, you're putting your offerings before a wide audience—wider than any individual dealer could deliver. And if you have rarities or highly desirable items to auction, it takes only two people obsessed with adding a particular prize to their collections to drive the bidding higher than what you could hope to realize from most other sources.

The All-Important Description

An honest, compelling description—complete with good-quality photographs—is essential to a successful sale, whether by a published ad or an Internet auction. Interested buyers scan a great many ads and click through long lists of page views quickly. If your description doesn't catch their eye, or if it leaves them with obvious unanswered questions, they're likely to move on. Consider the following examples.

Poorly written descriptions:

Plastic Umbrella Stand with Holes

This vintage plastic umbrella stand has 10 holes for umbrellas and is in good condition. You will not be disappointed with this item.

Vintage Funky 60's Kartell Chair

Good condition

Well-written descriptions:

Artemide Dedalo Umbrella Stand—'60s Pop Design

Emma Gismondi-Schweinberger designed this vintage umbrella stand for Artemide in the late 1960s. Standing 15" tall and measuring 14" in diameter, this fabulous Italian pop design is in excellent condition with no chips, cracks, or discoloration. It's embossed on the underside with the Artemide logo and the designer name. Satisfaction guaranteed.

Vintage Kartell Chair, Style 4850

Designed by Giorgina Castiglioni, Giorgio Garivaghi, and Aldo Lanza, 1965.

This example was produced between 1970 and 1973.

Orange ABS with black rubber foot pads, 28" tall.

Overall good, clean condition with slight fading around feet, 3" stress mark at top base of chair back.

Molded mark under seat, "KARTELL Designer: Castiglioni, Garivaghi, Lanza Made in USA by Beylerian Ltd."

Documented in L'Utopie du Tout Plastique, page 59.

Emma Gismondi-Schweinberger's Dedalo umbrella stand, Dedalotto vase, and Dedalino pencil holder, for Artemide (Italy), 1966. *Photo courtesy of designaddict.com.*

Before you start posting your items for sale on the Internet, it's a good idea to do some online research. Search completed auctions for comparable items to see how they are described and the kinds of prices they are fetching.

You Want to Become a Dealer

Many collectors who've acquired a lot of pieces eventually consider becoming a dealer. And why not? What better way is there to make an income than by dabbling in something you're passionate about?

But being a dealer isn't as easy as printing business cards and renting a table or booth at a show. There are many considerations, including accumulating and storing inventory, tagging items, making arrangements for shows (reserving booth space, accommodations, travel, and so on), signing leases for space in mall venues, and writing and placing ads—not to mention your legal obligations to state and federal tax authorities. Read an introductory book about running a small business, or consult with a small-business counselor before you take this route. Make sure that you really want to do it before you get in too deep. If you decide to try it, there are a number of ways you can go.

Shows

You've undoubtedly had great times attending shows as a collector. But as a dealer, be prepared for an arduous experience. First, there's the red tape of renting table or booth space (which may not be easily available to newcomers or may be in the most undesirable locations). Realize, too, that you'll have to pack and transport your inventory to the show site. Then there's the "load-in" and setup, which is usually the day before the show or at the crack of dawn the day of the show. Be prepared for physical labor, long hours, and a substantial cash outlay before your first customer even steps into your booth.

Is it worth it? If you end up with a profit after you've covered your investment in inventory and all of your expenses, consider it a great show. Then the fringe benefits of hotel "room hopping," buying and selling with other dealers before opening, learning more about the field, and making new contacts become dividends to offset all the time and hard work you've put into the show.

Malls

Antiques-and-collectibles malls offer a number of advantages to sellers. They're a kind of "long-term show" in that most of the people who come through their doors are dealers or collectors, who may be looking for specific pieces or just browsing. Depending on the mall, you may be obliged to pay only the rental fee for your space or display case plus a commission on sales. Other malls expect you to put in time as part of your contract. You may also be expected to rotate your stock periodically to keep the mall's inventory looking fresh.

What's the downside to selling your collection at a mall? Your merchandise can get lost among the hundreds of display cases. Most malls offer general collectible merchandise, so the number of '60s and '70s collectors coming through the door may be relatively small compared with more targeted venues.

In the worst-case scenario, you may find at the end of your mall lease that you sold little or nothing. In the meantime, your investment has just been sitting there. That's why seasoned dealers use different sales venues simultaneously. They may be attending shows, stocking a mall case, selling online, or even putting up items at live auctions—all at the same time.

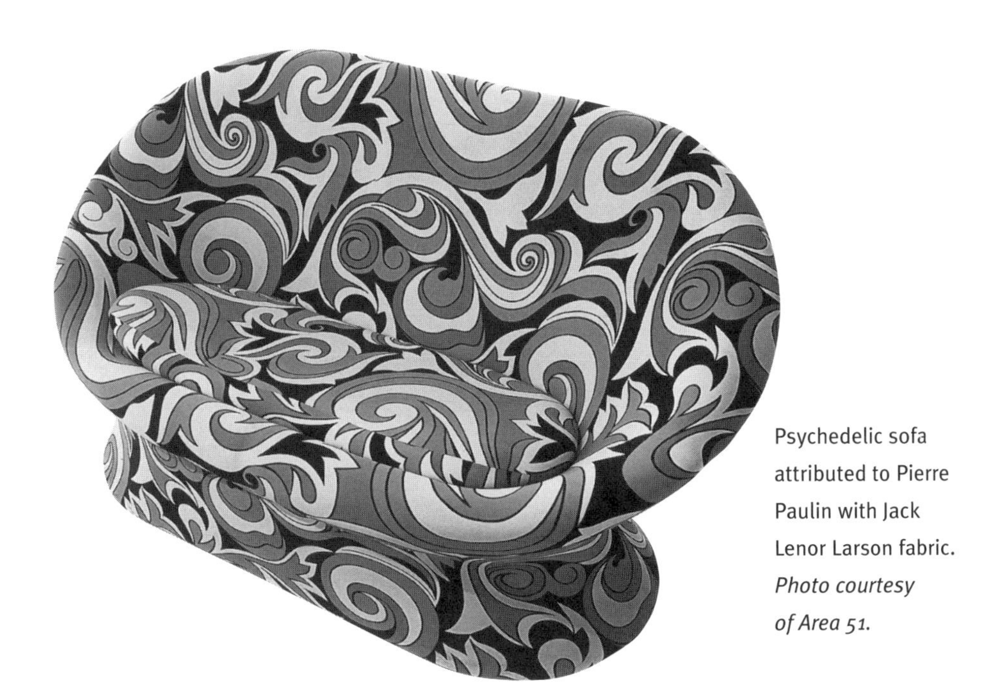

Psychedelic sofa attributed to Pierre Paulin with Jack Lenor Larson fabric. *Photo courtesy of Area 51.*

Live Auctions

Live auctions are quite different from online auctions in that you're putting your pieces in the hands of a professional auctioneer. Auctions are sometimes held in association with club shows. In those cases, one of the club officers may act as the auctioneer.

Your concerns with live auctions should be:

- **Is the auctioneer reputable?** He should be a member of a recognized auctioneers' association.
- **Where does he advertise, and how effectively?** The results of a live auction depend entirely on the turnout of bidders.
- **Does the auctioneer publish a catalog?** High-end auctions are generally cataloged. Auctioneers who produce catalogs likely have extensive mailing lists to solicit interested collectors.
- **How will the items be sold?** Depending on what you have to sell, you may want the most desirable pieces to be sold individually, with the more common ones grouped in lots.
- **What's the commission?** Auctioneers usually charge a percentage of the winning bid. If you have a large collection to auction, you may be able to negotiate the commission. It never hurts to ask.

Advertising and Mail-Order Selling

You may want to try placing ads in collectors' magazines or collectibles trade papers. If so, your description will be all-important, as this is generally a two-step selling process. Here's how it works: If your ads are well written, they'll generate correspondence from people who want to know more. When that happens, you must be ready to send them a more detailed description and photo (a digital image if you're using the Internet) of the items in which they're interested. You may hear back from some of them a second time with more questions or, if you're lucky, start preliminary negotiations on a purchase.

A word to the wise: It's a good idea to protect your private address by listing only your name, a post-office-box address, phone number, and e-mail address in your ads.

If you're simply selling items from your collection as a sideline, mail order can be a distracting way to do business. You'll get phone calls and voice-mail messages at all times of day and night, and you'll end up playing phone tag with callbacks. You have a lot of work to do, both on the phone and at the post office, to get information to people and follow through on sales. That's why most successful mail-order dealers advertise repeatedly and set themselves up to make this a primary sales avenue.

Dealing with One of Life's Certainties

If you've been a little lax about record keeping as a collector, you can't afford to make the same mistake as a dealer—whether you're selling by mail order, online, at shows, or in malls. As a seller of any kind, you're dealing with state and federal tax authorities.

Your inventory should include—at the least—a description of each item, the documented price you paid for it, and the year in which you purchased it. The IRS is interested in any profit you realize over what you originally paid for the item plus the expenses you incurred in selling it. If you paid to have an item repaired or restored, factor in that cost too.

It's best to consult with your tax professional or accountant before you set out as a dealer. He or she will be able to counsel you on the details of your individual situation so you'll comply with the law. Your numbers person may also be able to give you some pointers to help minimize the amount of tax you'll owe at the end of the year. He or she can help you apply for a tax ID (or resale) number and explain why that may be a good idea.

Donating Your Collection

Depending on your situation, donating your collection to an organization or institution may be your best financial move, or, at least, one that has certain tax advantages. You will have to get the collection appraised in order to qualify for a tax deduction, and of course your gift must be to a qualified nonprofit entity, such as a museum or historical society. Your tax professional will be able to guide you through the tax-compliance details relating to gifts of property.

Most important, make sure that you are emotionally ready to part with your collection. You might be able to visit your former collection in its new home, but once it's donated, you can never take it back.

A combination of cool plastic and comfortable upholstery, this ca. 1970 lounge chair was designed by Steen Ostergaard for Cado of Denmark. *Photos courtesy of Area 51.*

RESOURCES TO FURTHER YOUR COLLECTING

Shows

Brimfield Antique Show

Route 20
Brimfield, MA 01010
E-mail: lmyers@tiac.net
Web site: www.brimfield.com

Comments: This is arguably the largest outdoor show of its kind in the country, with more than five thousand dealers selling collectibles of all descriptions. It runs for approximately one week three times a year, in May, July, and September. Several individual promoters run concurrent shows in different fields located on both sides of a small road in the Massachusetts countryside. The Web site is extremely informative, with everything from a dealer locator to helpful hints on what to bring and what to wear. Know your stuff if you visit Brimfield, because the selling can be fast and furious.

Manhattan Antiques & Collectibles
Triple Pier Expo
Passenger Ship Terminal Piers 88, 90, and 92
West 48th to 55th Streets and 12th Avenue in Manhattan
Presented by Stella Show Management
147 West 24th Street
New York, NY 10011
Telephone: 212-255-0020
Fax: 212-255-0002
E-mail: stellashows@aol.com
Web site: www.stellashows.com

Comments: This show usually takes place in March and November on sequential weekends, with the first weekend getting the biggest buzz. Three separate piers chock-full of various types of antiques and collectibles make this a not-to-be-missed event for several collecting interests. Pier 88 is the one to concentrate on for twentieth-century antiques, including '60s and '70s items.

Miami Modernism Show
Radisson Deauville Resort
6701 Collins Avenue
Miami, FL 33141
Presented by Caussin Productions
43½ North Saginaw
Pontiac, MI 48342
Telephone: 248-334-9660
Fax: 248-253-1883
E-mail: jcaussin@aol.com
Web site: www.miamimodernism.com

Comments: Features high-end collectibles from all eras of the twentieth century, including '60s and '70s design. One of the premiere shows for twentieth-century modern. Held in January each year.

Michigan Modernism Exposition
Southfield Civic Center
26000 Evergreen
Southfield, MI 48037
Presented by M&M Enterprises
19946 Great Oaks Circle South
Clinton Township, MI 48036-4401
Telephone: 810-469-1706 *or* 810-465-9441
Fax: 810-468-5694
E-mail: mandminfo@aol.com
Web site: www.antiqnet.com/M&M

Comments: A show with a wide range of twentieth-century modern collectibles, including '60s and '70s items. This show takes place each spring and enjoys a good following, with some of the better dealers around the country in attendance.

Specialist Dealers

A&J 20th Century Design
Ana Azevedo and Jerry Hilden
255 Lafayette Street
New York, NY 10012
Telephone: 212-226-6290
E-mail: info@a-j20thcentury.com
Web site: www.a-j20thcentury.com

Comments: A tiny Soho shop filled to the ceiling with '60s and '70s design. Although the shop has a Web site, you'll want to visit the bricks-and-mortar location to see the vintage gems they always seem to have.

Art & Industrial Design
399 Lafayette Street
New York, NY 10003
Telephone: 212-477-0116
Fax: 212-477-1420

Comments: Probably the largest collection of modernism under one roof. Better than a museum because you can actually buy the stuff!

Cherry
185 Orchard Street
New York, NY 10002
Telephone: 212-358-7131

Comments: You never know what will turn up here, but the owners have a great eye for '60s and '70s design and fashions.

Galleria Modernariato
Corso Vittorio Emanuele
Angolo Via San Paolo, 1
20122 Milan
Italy
Telephone: 39-02-86-90-948
Fax: 39-02-87-59-72
E-mail: info@modernariato.it
Web site: www.modernariato.it

Comments: If you have pockets deep enough to acquire some truly rare and unique items, this is the place for you.

Mode Moderne
159 North Third Street
Philadelphia, PA 19106
Telephone: 215-627-0299
Fax: 215-627-1499
E-mail: ModeModern@aol.com
Web site: www.modemoderne.com

Comments: A great shop for design with a pedigree. Both the Web site and shop are terrific places to find an interesting selection of '60s and '70s items, with the occasional rare piece showing up.

Pop / Atomic
E-mail: gomod@aol.com
Web site: www.gomod.com/popatomic.htm

Comments: A shop available only on the Web, where the focus is on '50s-to-'70s design, with heavy emphasis on '60s items.

Two examples of modular furnishings: a room divider designed by Pierluigi Spadolini and Paolo Felli for Kartell (Italy) in 1969, and three sections (of four) from a Quattroquarti table and shelves designed by Rodolfo Bonetto for Bernini (Italy) in 1970. *Photo courtesy of Erica George Dines.*

Retromodern.com
805 Peachtree
Atlanta, GA 30308
Telephone: 404-724-0093
Fax: 404-724-0424
E-mail: mail@retromodern.com
Web site: www.retromodern.com

Comments: The Web site offers a strong selection of vintage and current production '60s and '70s design.

Simplymod.com

E-mail: meyecul@aol.com

Web site: www.simplymod.com

Comments: An Internet-only dealer with a constantly changing selection of '60s and '70s design. Everything from high design to kitsch, with many European items.

Auction Houses and Auctions

Christie's London, South Kensington

85 Old Brompton Road
London, SW7 3LD
England
Telephone: 0171-581-7611
Fax: 0171-321-3321
E-mail: info@christies.com
Web site: www.christies.com

Comments: Christie's hosts a biannual modern-design auction whose catalogs are a must for your resource library.

David Rago Auctions

333 North Main Street
Lambertville, NJ 08530
Telephone: 609-397-9374
Fax: 609-397-9377
E-mail: suggestions@ragoarts.com
Web site: www.ragoarts.com

Comments: These quarterly modern-design auctions always include some examples of '60s and '70s design. They're a favorite with dealers.

Los Angeles Modern Auctions
P.O. Box 462006
Los Angeles, CA 90046
Telephone: 323-904-1950
Fax: 323-904-1954
E-mail: peter@lamodern.com
Web site: www.lamodern.com

Comments: Holds quarterly modern-design auctions as well as smaller monthly design auctions. This Los Angeles auction house also has an online catalog where you can preview the upcoming auction and see results from those that have concluded.

Treadway Gallery
2029 Madison Road
Cincinnati, OH 45208
Telephone: 513-321-6742
Fax: 513-871-7722
E-mail: info@treadwaygallery.com
Web site: www.treadwaygallery.com

Comments: Treadway Gallery holds several modern-design auctions annually, with a nice representation of '60s and '70s decor. Its catalogs and publications are always in demand as references on the pricing of specific items.

Wright
1140 West Fulton
Chicago, IL 60607
Telephone: 312-563-0020
Fax: 312-563-0040
E-mail: wright20@earthlink.net
Web site: www.wright20.com

Comments: The Wright auctions are quite strong in higher caliber merchandise. Their publications look and read more like books than auction catalogs.

Trade Magazines

Echoes

P.O. Box 155
Cummaquid, MA 02637
Telephone: 508-362-3822 *or* 800-695-5768
Fax: 508-362-6670
E-mail: hey@deco-echoes.com
Web site: www.deco-echoes.com

Comments: A quarterly magazine devoted to modern design in general and a very good source of information on '60s and '70s collectibles. Features include home interiors decorated with period furnishings, fashions, and informational articles. Many of the shops selling the merchandise are also advertisers, and this makes it a great resource for locating shops in your area as well.

The Modernism Magazine

333 North Main Street
Lambertville, NJ 08530
Telephone: 609-397-4104
Fax: 609-397-9377
E-mail: modernist@ragoarts.com
Web site: www.ragoarts.com/nj/modsub.html

Comments: This quarterly magazine devoted to twentieth-century design comes from the same people who conduct the Rago Auctions. Well-respected author Cara Greenberg is the managing editor.

Online Auctions, Marketers, and Web Sites

Amazon.com and eBay.com

Web sites: www.amazon.com and www.ebay.com

Comments: Both online auctions can be good places to find '60s and '70s design objects. Be aware that many companies such as Target and Ikea are currently producing items that appear to be from this period, so review the seller's feedback before bidding. Helpful search terms are panton, op art, Italian plastic, jvc videosphere, panapet, eero aarnio, and joe colombo.

Deco-echoes.com

Web site: www.deco-echoes.com

Comments: This site features classified ads, an online catalog, resources section, shop listing, discussion board, and information about *Echoes* magazine.

Design Addict

E-mail: contact@designaddict.com

Web site: www.designaddict.com

Comments: A resource site with exhibits, links, and information on modern design.

Massimo Vignelli Nuts and Bolts bottle for Colton (U.S.A.), 4¼" high, plastic and glass, 1968. This men's toiletry bottle is one in a series Vignelli designed. *Photo courtesy of Fremont Antique Mall.*

GoMod

E-mail: mail@gomod.com

Web site: www.gomod.com

Comments: This Web portal links to many of the best twentieth-century-design Web sites, including those concentrating on '60s and '70s.

Tribu Design

E-mail: contact@tribu-design.com

Web site: www.tribu-design.com

Comments: Archives, links, and a database of furniture, lighting, and industrial design.

XXo

E-mail: xxo@worldnet.fr

Web site: www.xxo.com

Comments: This Paris-based site offers an outstanding array of '60s and '70s designs for sale or rent. If you are planning a trip to Paris, be sure to make contact in advance to arrange a visit.

E-groups

Design Addict Forums

Web site: www.designaddict.com/design-center/forums/forums-full.html

Comments: This site has two discussion boards, one for design topics and the other for identification of objects.

Mid-Century Modern List

Web site: www.egroups.com/group/midcenturymodern

Comments: This popular discussion list with more than three hundred members discusses issues relating to designs from 1925 to 1975.

Vico Magistretti's Vicario (1971) and Selene (1969) chairs for Artemide accompany Giotto Stoppino's 4905 nesting tables (1968) for Kartell. A sleek Pelota lamp from 1971, designed by Studio D.A. for Lamperti, rounds out this group of Italian designs. *Photo courtesy of Erica George Dines.*

Museums and Galleries

Cooper-Hewitt National Design Museum
Smithsonian Institution
2 East 91st Street
New York, NY 10128-0606
Telephone: 212-849-8400
E-mail: publicinfo@ch.si.edu
Web site: www.si.edu/ndm

Denver Art Museum
100 West 14th Avenue Parkway
Denver, CO 80204-2788
Telephone: 720-865-5000
E-mail: web-mail@denverartmuseum.org
Web site: www.denverartmuseum.org

Montreal Museum of Decorative Arts
2200 Crescent Street
P.O. Box 1200, Station A
Montreal, Quebec
H3C 2Y9 Canada
Telephone: 514-284-1252
Fax: 514-284-0123
Web site: www.madm.org

The Museum of Modern Art (MOMA)
11 West 53rd Street
New York, NY 10019
Telephone: 212-708-9400
Web site: www.moma.org

Plasticarium
Locquenghien Street 35
1000 Brussels, Belgium
Web site: www.fiftie-fiftie.be/plastic.htm

Vitra
Web site: www.design-museum.com

Vitra Design Museum Weil am Rhein
Charles-Eames-Strasse 1
D-79576 Weil am Rhein
Germany
E-mail: info@design-museum.de

Vitra Design Museum Berlin
Kopenhagener Strasse 58
D-10437 Berlin/Prenzlaner Berg
Germany
E-mail: mateo.kries@design-museum.de

Libraries

Cooper-Hewitt National Design Museum Branch Library
Smithsonian Institution
2 East 91st Street
New York, NY 10128-0606
Telephone: 212-849-8331
Fax: 212-849-8339
E-mail: libmail@sil.si.edu
Web site: www.sil.si.edu/Branches/chm-hp.htm

Comments: You must make an appointment to visit the library, but can search online for publications located at the library and at all Smithsonian-affiliated libraries.

The Museum of Modern Art (MOMA)
11 West 53rd Street
New York, NY 10019
Telephone: 212-708-9433
Fax: 212-333-1122
E-mail: library@moma.org
Web site: http://library.moma.org

Comments: You must make an appointment to visit the library, but can search the catalog online.

Ball calendar, ca. 1974. *Photo courtesy of Fremont Antique Mall.*

Our thanks to the following photo contributors:

Area 51
401 East Pine Street
Seattle, WA 98122
Telephone: 206-568-4782

Design Addict
E-mail: contact@designaddict.com
Web site: www.designaddict.com

Erica George Dines Photography
Atlanta, GA

Fremont Antique Mall
3419 Fremont Place North
Seattle, WA 98103
Telephone: 206-548-9140

Wright
1140 West Fulton
Chicago, IL 60607
Telephone: 312-563-0020
Web site: www.wright20.com

REPRESENTATIVE VALUE GUIDE

We asked contributors on both sides of the Atlantic to compile a brief listing of items and their values in several collected design and decor categories. This sampling will provide the newcomer with a sense of both the range of material available and the prices. Some items will be more readily found in Europe; many are relatively common in the U.S.; and we've noted some that are still in production. A few are true rarities—as the prices reflect. For the purposes of this listing, assume that prices apply to items in very good to excellent condition, with minor wear—if any—and no objectionable fading, discoloration, or deterioration of materials.

Item	Manufacturer	Designer	Dimensions	Pattern or Color	Value in $
Seats					
Elda armchair	Comfort	Joe Colombo	36.5" high	Black and white	1,800–2,200
Selene chair	Artemide	Vico Magistretti	29.5" x 19.75" x 18.5"	Green or red	240–280
Egg garden chair	Reuter Product	Peter Ghyczy	17.75" x 29.5" x 33"	Yellow or red	1,500–1,800
Cantilever chair	Herman Miller	Verner Panton	32.5" high		400–500
Blow inflatable chair	Zanotta	Gionatan De Pas, Donato D'Urbino, Paolo Lomazzi	39.5" x 39.5" x 23.5"	Clear/transparent	600–725
Vicario armchair	Artemide	Vico Magistretti	27" x 28" x 27"	Green	450–500
Tables					
Giano Vano end table	Artemide	Emma Gismondi-Schweinberger	16" high	Orange	280–340
Boomerang desk	Leleu-Deshay	Maurice Calka	70" wide	White	19,000–23,000
Amanta coffee table	B&B	Mario Bellini	13.75" x 27" x 27"	White	280–340
Demetrio 45 stacking table	Artemide	Vico Magistretti	17.5" x 17.5" x 9"	Orange	175–225
Kantarelli dining table	Asko	Eero Aarnio	50" diameter x 28" high	White	1,250–1,500
Quattroquarti sectional table	Bernini	Rodolfo Bonetto	48" diameter x 12" high	Red	400–500

Item	Manufacturer	Designer	Dimensions	Pattern or Color	Value in $
Bedroom Furniture					
Double bed	Prisunic	Marc Held	82.5" x 90.5" x 15"	White	1,800–2,100
4550 single bed	Kartell	Anna Castelli Ferrieri and Ignazio Gardella		Red	1,500–1,800
Centipede single bed	Kartell	Antonio Locatelli and Pietro Salmoiraghi		White	1,700–2,000
Chapter 1 triple dresser	Broyhill	Unknown	62" x 18" x 29.5"		800–1,000
Man's wardrobe	CEI, France	Raymond Loewy			2,500–3,000
Storage and Display					
Wall All 1-wall organizer	M Design	Dorothée Maurer Becker	34.25" x 26"	Green	310–350
Display shelves	Rodier	Unknown	82" high	White	700–800
4907 wall-mount shelf	Kartell	Marcello Siard	31" x 12" x 13.75"	Red	200–250
Round-Up stacking unit	Kartell	Anna Castelli Ferrieri	12.5" diameter x 15.5" high	Red	150–175
4925-4940 modular four-shelf unit	Kartell	Olaf von Bohr	32.5" x 11" x 73.5"	Red	600–750
Lamps and Lighting					
Chiara floor lamp	Flos	Mario Bellini	57.5" x 28" x 20"	Chrome	1,500–1,800
KD 27 stackable table lamp	Kartell	Joe Colombo	9.5" x 9.5"	Orange	250–300
Arco floor lamp (in production)	Flos	Achille and Pier Giacomo Castiglioni	78.5" (max. extension 95")	Chrome, marble base	1,500–1,800
Flower Pot hanging light	Louis Poulsen	Verner Panton	8.75" diameter	Chrome	350–400
Electronics					
"Pop" record player	Minerva	Mario Bellini	8.5" x 8" x 3"	Orange	350–400
Television	Teleavia	Roger Tallon	15.25" x 20.5" x 11.75"	White and black	700–850
Ariante fan	Vortice	Marco Zanuso	7" x 7" x 4"	Red	190–210
Panapet portable AM radio	Panasonic		4" diameter	Blue	35–45
Videosphere television	JVC		11" diameter x 13" high	White	300–375
TR-005 Orbitel television	Panasonic		11" x 10" x 10"	Silver	600–725

Item	Manufacturer	Designer	Dimensions	Pattern or Color	Value in $
Decorative Accessories					
Glass vase	Vistosi	Ettore Sottsass		Blue and green	2,200–2,500
Glass vase	Carlo Moretti	Carlo Moretti	8" high	Chartreuse	150–170
Bag ceramic vase	Rosenthal	Tapio Wirkkala	7.75" high	Light brown	115–125
Spyros ashtray	Artemide	Eleonore Peduzzi Riva	8.5" x 8.5" x 1"	White with black ball	275–325
Dedalo umbrella stand	Artemide	Emma Gismondi-Schweinberger	15" diameter x 13" high	White	175–225
Tableware					
Bomba plastic dinnerware (set)	Villeroy & Boch	Helen von Boch and Federico Fabbrini		Orange	550–650
Smoke stem glass (in production)	Arnolfo di Cambio	Joe Colombo	Various	Clear	100–110
Gres line teapot	Ceramica Franco Pozzi	Ambrogio Pozzi		White	180–210
Beverage pitcher	Heller	Massimo Vignelli	5" x 7.5" x 8.25"	Magenta	75–90
Set=9 beverage set		Jean-Pierre Vitrac	8.5" x 5" x 10"	Orange	100–125
Plateau Amuse-Gueule (Molecular biscuit/hors d'oeuvres server)		Yonel Lebovici	15.5" diameter	White	250–325
Kitchenware and Countertop Appliances					
Set of containers 7301, 7302, 7303, 7304	Kartell	Anna Castelli Ferrieri	6.25", 7.5", 8.75", 11" high	Red	300–320
KSM 1 coffee grinder	Braun	Reinhold Weiss	6.75" x 3.25"	Black	120–130
Kitchen scale	Terraillon	Marco Zanuso	6.5" x 4. 25" x 4.75"	Yellow and black	40–45
Quattrefoil bowl with compartments	Heller	Massimo and Lella Vignelli	16" x 16" x 4.25"	Yellow	150–200
Folding breakfast tray	Kartell	Olaf von Bohr	23" x 15" x 9"	Red	75–100
Graphic Art					
Onde screen print	Danese	Enzo Mari	26.75" x 26.75"	White and black	1,400–1,500
Pony chair ad	Asko	Eero Aarnio	33.75" x 49.25"	Brown and white	400–500
Perpetual wall calendar	Piranha	Jean-Pierre Vitrac	19" x 19"	White and black	500–650
Spectrum: op-art fabric wall hanging	Mira-X	Verner Panton	48" x 48"	Orange, yellow, brown, rust	350–425
Inflatable pillow		Peter Max	12" x 12"	Various	40–50

GLOSSARY

ART CENTER COLLEGE OF DESIGN LIBRARY

ABS Acrylonitrile-butadiene-styrene, a rigid opaque plastic most commonly used for injection molding.

fiberglass Glass-reinforced polyester covered with a slick resin gel coat. A popular component in many designs of the era, it usually was used for large furniture pieces that required greater strength than other plastics could offer.

Lucite, Perspex, Plexiglas Trademarks for clear or tinted translucent, acrylic plastic.

melamine Dense, rigid plastic that is resistant to heat; often used for tableware and ashtrays.

op art Abbreviation for "optical art," one of the most important visual movements of the '60s. Op art is an abstract form characterized by the use of straight or curved lines or geometric patterns often to create illusory effects, such as motion. Victor Vasarely is perhaps its most famous exponent.

plastics Many of the most recognizable designs from the '60s are made of plastic. The various types include ABS (acrylonitrile-butadiene-styrene), GRP (glass-reinforced polyester), PP (polypropylene), PMMA (polymethyl methacrylate), PS (polystyrene), and PVC (polyvinyl chloride).

polypropylene A soft plastic with a "waxy" finish.

pop art Art in which commonplace objects are used as subject matter and often incorporated into the work.

"was white" A term used by collectors to describe the discoloration of plastic objects that were originally stark white.

RECOMMENDED BOOKS

Ambasz, Emilio, ed. *Italy: The New Domestic Landscape; Achievements and Problems of Italian Design.* New York: Museum of Modern Art, 1972.
Comments: This catalog from the landmark exhibition at MOMA is out of print; however, you might be able to find it on eBay or through a book retailer.

Arnoldsche Art Publications. *Plastics and Design.* Wappinger's Falls, N.Y.: Antique Collectors Club, 1998.
Comments: A beautifully illustrated book on the history of the use of plastic in design from 1900 to the present. Look for it at specialty art and design bookstores.

Decelle, Philippe, Diane Hennebert, and Pierre Loze. *L'Utopie du Tout Plastique 1960–1973.* Brussels: Fondation pour l'Architecture, 1994.
Comments: A bible for collectors of the period. This book is out of print; however, it frequently shows up on eBay.

Fiell, Charlotte, and Peter Fiell, eds. *Decorative Art 1960's* and *Decorative Art 1970's.* Cologne: Taschen, 2000.

Garner, Philippe. *Sixties Design.* London: Taschen, 1996.
Comments: An overview of styles of the period, with lots of photos.

Greenberg, Cara. *Op to Pop: Furniture of the 1960s.* Boston: Bullfinch Press, 1999.
Comments: An excellent crash course in the best of furniture design and a who's who of designers.

Jackson, Lesley. *The Sixties: Decade of Design Revolution.* London: Phaidon Press, 1998.
Comments: A comprehensive overview of the styles and trends of the decade.

Morello, Augusto, and Anna Castelli Ferrieri. *Plastic and Design.* Vol. 2 of *From Project to Product.* Milan: Arcadis, 1988.

Vitra Design Museum. *Verner Panton: The Collected Works.* Vitra Design Museum Publications, 2001.
Comments: This book can be purchased through the Vitra Design Museum Web site at www.design-museum.com.

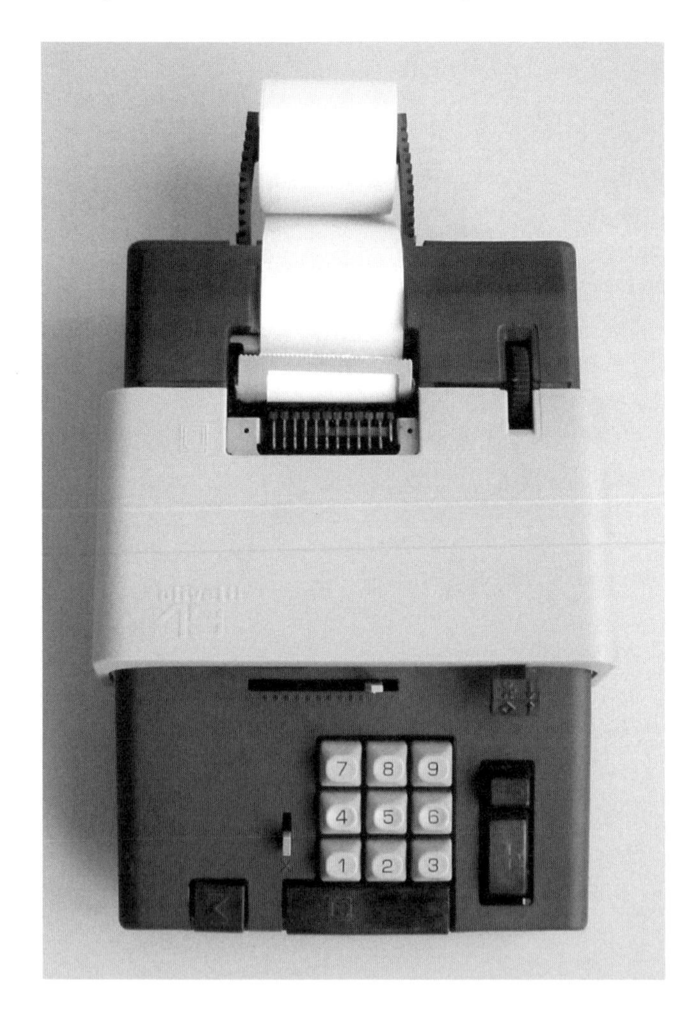

Ettore Sottsass's Summa 19 calculator for Olivetti (Italy). *Photo courtesy of designaddict.com.*

ABOUT THE INTERNATIONAL SOCIETY OF APPRAISERS

The Collector's Compass series is endorsed by the International Society of Appraisers, one of North America's leading non-profit associations of professionally educated and certified personal-property appraisers. Members of the ISA include many of the industry's most respected independent appraisers, auctioneers, and dealers. ISA appraisers specialize in more than two hundred areas of expertise in four main specialty pathways: antiques and residential contents, fine art, gems and jewelry, and machinery and equipment.

Established in 1979 and consisting of more than 1,375 members, the ISA is founded on two core principles: to educate its members through a wide range of continuing education and training opportunities, and to promote and maintain the highest ethical and professional standards in the field of appraisals.

Education through the ISA

In conjunction with the University of Maryland University College, the ISA offers a series of post-secondary professional courses in appraisal studies, including a two-level certification program.

The ISA recognizes three membership levels within its organization—Associate Member, Accredited Member, and Certified Member—with educational programs in place for achieving higher distinctions within the society. ISA members who complete the required coursework are recognized with the title of Certified Appraiser of Personal Property (CAPP). Through its pioneering education programs, the ISA plays a vital role in producing qualified appraisers with a professional education in appraisal theory, principles, procedures, ethics, and law as it pertains to personal-property appraisal.

Professional Standards of the ISA

The ISA is dedicated to the highest ethical standards of conduct, ensuring public confidence in the ability and qualifications of its members. To help members perform their work with the most up-to-date knowledge of professional standards, the ISA is continually updating, expanding, and improving its courses and criteria of conduct.

For more information about the International Society of Appraisers, contact its corporate offices:

Toll-free: 800-472-4732
E-mail: ISAHQ@isa-appraisers.org
Web site: www.isa-appraisers.org

ABOUT THE CONTRIBUTORS

Barry Bryant has been on a continual collecting spree for the past nine years. Beginning his collection with a kitschy 1950s lime-green ballerina lamp, this one-time pharmacist was on his way toward finding a new career—although his success might have been difficult to predict at the start. After setting up a booth at an antiques show years ago, only one item sold, and thoughts of business success were dashed. Later stints in three different antiques malls were semisuccessful, but when Mr. Bryant launched his GoMod.com Web site in 1998, it began to appear that the dream of "hobby as career" finally was a possibility. Initially developed as a site to sell off collection overflow, it quickly developed into a destination site for collectors of twentieth-century design. With the success of this site and the help of his longtime partner John McLendon, Mr. Bryant finally threw in the mortar and pestle after fourteen years and embarked on his dream. He can be reached through the GoMod Web site or at (877) 56-GO-MOD.

Karl Taps is a native New Yorker who just couldn't get enough of hunting the flea markets and vintage shops. A seasoned collector of a wide range of modern decorative arts, Mr. Taps found his professional niche in the radical designs of 1980s postmodernism. Staying a step ahead of the pack, he launched BanalDesign.com in 1998, the first Web site devoted exclusively to the collecting of postmodern design. Karl Taps can be contacted through BanalDesign.com or at 800-515-3186.

Christopher J. Kuppig has spent his entire career in book publishing. For several years he directed programs at Dell Publishing, Consumer Reports Books, and most recently Chilton Book Company—where his assignments included managing the Wallace-Homestead and Warman's lines of antiques-and-collectibles guides.

In 1997, Mr. Kuppig founded Stone Studio Publishing Services, a general management consultancy to book publishers. Acting as series editor for the Collector's Compass series has given him the opportunity to draw upon his wide-ranging network of contacts in the collecting field.

Mr. Kuppig resides with his wife and three children in eastern Massachusetts.

Art Center College of Design
Library
1700 Lida Street
Pasadena, Calif. 91103

INDEX

Note: Page numbers in italics indicate information in a photo or caption.

ART CENTER COLLEGE OF DESIGN LIBRARY

17 Oct. 2006 Art Consulting: Scandinavia 14.50 100404